TRANSFORMED *in His* PRESENCE

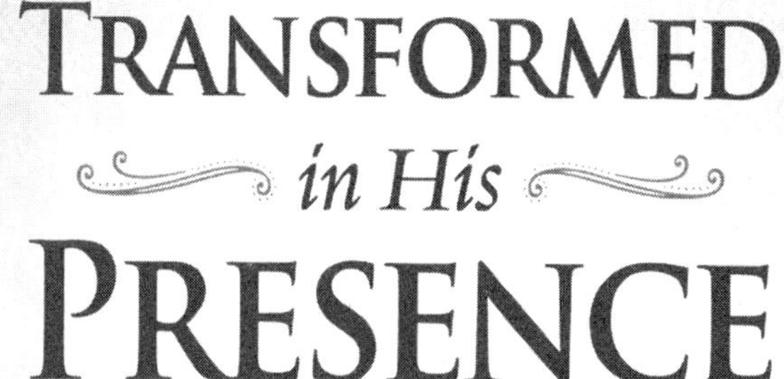

Transformed in His Presence

Francis Frangipane

Charisma House

Most Charisma House Book Group products are available at special quantity discounts for bulk purchase for sales promotions, premiums, fund-raising, and educational needs. For details, write Charisma House Book Group, 600 Rinehart Road, Lake Mary, Florida 32746, or telephone (407) 333-0600.

Transformed in His Presence
by Francis Frangipane
Published by Charisma House
Charisma Media/Charisma House Book Group
600 Rinehart Road
Lake Mary, Florida 32746
www.charismahouse.com

Cover design by Vincent Pirozzi
Design Director: Justin Evans

Visit the author's website at www.frangipane.org.

Library of Congress Cataloging-in-Publication Data:
An application to register this book for cataloging has been submitted to the Library of Congress.
International Standard Book Number: 978-1-62999-482-6
E-book ISBN: 978-1-62999-483-3

Portions of this book were previously published by Charisma House as *Holiness, Truth, and the Presence of God*, ISBN 978-1-61638-203-2, copyright © 2011; *When the Many Are One*, ISBN 978-1-59979-529-4, copyright © 1991, 2009; and *The Shelter of the Most High*, ISBN 978-1-59979-281-1, copyright © 2008.

18 19 20 21 22 — 987654321
Printed in the United States of America

Day 1
True Holiness

Then the Lord said to him, "Now you Pharisees clean the outside of the cup and the dish. But inside you are full of extortion and wickedness."
—Luke 11:39

The holiness we are seeking goes much deeper than merely cleaning the outside of our cup (Luke 11:39). We are not seeking an antidote that deals with the effects but not the cause of our human condition. We are seeking the living God, for true holiness does not come from following rules; it comes from following Christ.

The path toward true holiness, therefore, is a path full of both life and death, perils and blessings. It is a path upon which you will be challenged, empowered, provoked, and crucified. But you will not be disappointed. If it is God you seek, it is God you will find.

My Spiritual Preparation for Today

Day 2
Holiness and Humility

Woe to you, Pharisees! For you tithe mint and rue and every herb and pass over justice and the love of God. These you ought to have done, without leaving the others undone.
—Luke 11:42

Jesus did not condemn sinners; He condemned hypocrites, people who excuse their own sins while condemning the sins of another. They are not merely "two-faced," for even the best of us must work at single-mindedness in all instances. Hypocrites, therefore, refuse to admit they are, at times, two-faced, thereby pretending a righteousness that they fail to live.

Indeed, hypocrites do not discern their hypocrisy, for they cannot perceive flaws within themselves. Rarely do they actually deal with the corruption in their hearts. Since they seek no mercy, hypocrites have no mercy to give; since they are always under God's judgment, judging is what comes through them.

We cannot remain hypocrites and at the same time find holiness. Therefore, the first step we truly take toward sanctification is to admit we are not as holy as we would like to appear. This first step is called humility.

My Spiritual Preparation for Today

Day 3
Humility Brings Grace

Learn from Me. For I am meek and lowly in heart, and you will find rest for your souls.
—Matthew 11:29

The holiest, most powerful voice that ever spoke described Himself as "meek and lowly in heart." Why do we begin a journey to holiness and transformation with humility? Simply because holiness is the product of grace, and God gives grace only to the humble. And grace alone can change our hearts. Humility, therefore, is the substructure of transformation. It is the essence of all virtues.

At some point we will be confronted with the impurities of our hearts. The Holy Spirit reveals sinfulness, not to condemn us but to establish humility and deepen the knowledge of our need for grace. At this crossroad both holy men and hypocrites are bred. Those who become holy see their need and fall prostrate before God for deliverance. Those who become hypocrites are they who, in seeing their sin, excuse it and thus remain intact. Though all men must eventually stand at this junction, few are they who embrace the voice of truth; few are they who will walk humbly toward true holiness.

My Spiritual Preparation for Today

Day 4
Saving Grace

For God did not send His Son into the world to condemn the world, but that the world through Him might be saved.
—John 3:17

Hypocrites love to judge; it makes them feel superior. But it shall not be so with you. You must seek earnestly for lowliness of heart. Many zealous but proud Christians failed to reach holiness because they presumed they were called to judge others.

Jesus Christ did not come to condemn the world but to save the world. Anyone can pass judgment, but can they save? Can they lay down their lives in love, intercession, and faith for the one judged? Can they target an area of need and—rather than criticizing—fast and pray, asking God to supply the very virtue they feel is lacking? And then can they persevere in love-motivated prayer until that fallen area blooms in godliness? Such is the life Christ commands we follow!

To judge after the flesh requires but one eye and a carnal mind. On the other hand, it takes the loving faithfulness of Christ to redeem and save. One act of His love revealed through us will do more to warm cold hearts than the sum of all our pompous criticisms. Therefore, grow in love and excel in mercy, and you will have a clearer perception into the essence of holiness, for it is the nature of God, who is love.

My Spiritual Preparation for Today

Day 5
Judge Not

God demonstrates His own love toward us, in that while we were yet sinners, Christ died for us.
—Romans 5:8

If we are honestly pursuing our sanctification, we will soon discover we have no time for judging others. Indeed, being in need of mercy, we will seek eagerly for opportunities to be merciful to others.

Yes, Scripture tells us that Jesus judged men in certain situations, but His *motive* was always to save. His love was perfectly committed to the one He judged. When our love toward another is such that we can honestly say, like Christ, "I will never desert you, nor will I ever forsake you" (Heb. 13:5, NASB), our powers of discernment will be likewise perfected, for it is love alone that gives us pure motives in judgment (1 John 4:16–17).

Do you still insist on finding fault? Beware, Christ's standard of judgment is high: "He who is without sin among you, let him be the first to throw a stone" (John 8:7, NASB). Indeed, speak out against unrighteousness, but be motivated by the love of Jesus. Remember, it is written, "While we were yet sinners, Christ died for us" (Rom. 5:8). In the kingdom of God, unless you are first committed to die for people, you are not permitted to judge them.

My Spiritual Preparation for Today

Day 6

Are We Trying to Impress Men or God?

How can you believe, when you receive glory from one another and you do not seek the glory that is from the one and only God?
—John 5:44, NASB

If we are displaying our spirituality to impress men, still seeking honor from others, still living to appear righteous or special or "anointed" before people, can we honestly say we have been walking near to the living God? We know we are relating correctly to God when our hunger for His glory causes us to forsake the praise of men.

Does not all glory fade in the light of His glory? Even as Jesus challenged the genuineness of the Pharisees' faith, so He challenges us: "How can you believe, when you receive glory from one another?"

What a weak comfort is the praise of men. Upon such a frail ledge do we mortals build our happiness. Consider this: Was it not the same city whose songs and praise welcomed Jesus as "King...gentle, and mounted on a donkey" (Matt. 21:5–9, NASB) that roared, "Crucify Him!" less than one week later (Luke 23:21)? To seek the praise of men is to be tossed upon such a sea of instability!

My Spiritual Preparation for Today

Day 7
Seek the Glory of the Lord

He who speaks on his own authority seeks his own glory. But He who seeks the glory of Him who sent Him is true, and no unrighteousness is in Him.
—John 7:18

We must ask ourselves, whose glory do we seek in life, God's or our own? When we speak from ourselves and of ourselves, are we not seeking to solicit from men the praise that belongs only to God? To seek our glory is to fall headlong into vanity and deception, but the one who seeks the glory of the Lord is true. The same quality of heart that made Christ's intentions true must become our standard as well. For only to the degree that we are seeking the glory of God are our motivations true! Only to the degree that we abide in the glory of Him who sends us is there no unrighteousness in our hearts!

Therefore, let us give ourselves to seeking the glory of God, and let us do so until we find Him. As we behold the nature of Christ, as our eyes see *Him*, like Job we "abhor" ourselves and "repent in dust and ashes" (Job 42:6, kjv). As we are bathed in His glory, we shall be washed from seeking the glory of man.

My Spiritual Preparation for Today

Day 8
Finding God

You will seek Me and find Me when you search for Me with all your heart.
—Jeremiah 29:13, NASB

If we truly find Him, no one will have to tell us to be humble. No one need convince us our old natures are as filthy rags. As we truly find God, the things that are so highly esteemed among men will become detestable in our sight (Luke 16:15).

What could be more important than finding God? Take a day, a week, or a month and do nothing but seek Him, persisting until you find Him. Find God, and once you have Him, determine to live the rest of your life in pursuit of His glory. As you touch Him, something will come alive in you: something eternal, someone Almighty! Instead of looking down on people, you will seek to lift them up. You will dwell in the presence of God. And you will be holy, for *He* is holy.

My Spiritual Preparation for Today

Day 9
A Time to Seek

Seek the Lord and His strength; seek His face continually.
—1 Chronicles 16:11

There are certain times when the Lord calls us out of the routine of our daily lives. These are special seasons where His only command is "Seek My face." He has something precious and vitally important to give us that the familiar pattern of our daily devotions cannot accommodate. During such times people are often delivered of sins that have plagued them for years; others discover a depth in their walk with God that leads to greater effectiveness in ministry and prayer; still others experience breakthroughs in their families and are used by God to see loved ones brought into the kingdom.

My Spiritual Preparation for Today

Day 10
Seek God for Himself

Therefore if you have been raised up with Christ, keep seeking the things above, where Christ is, seated at the right hand of God. Set your mind on the things above, not on the things that are on earth. For you have died and your life is hidden with Christ in God. When Christ, who is our life, is revealed, then you also will be revealed with Him in glory.
—Colossians 3:1–4, NASB

We must seek God for Himself. Maturity starts as we break the cycle of seeking God only during hardship; holiness begins the moment we seek God for Himself. A touch from God is wonderful, but we are in pursuit of more than just an experience—more than "goose bumps and tears." We are seeking to abide with Christ, where we are continually aware of His fullness within us, where His presence dwells in us in glory.

My Spiritual Preparation for Today

Day 11
Follow the Lord Into the Unfamiliar

Now Moses used to take the tent and pitch it outside the camp, a good distance from the camp, and he called it the tent of meeting. And anyone who sought the LORD would go out to the tent of meeting which was outside the camp.
—Exodus 33:7, NASB

HOW DO WE enter the Lord's presence, the sacred place? Notice in the verse above that "anyone who sought the LORD would go out." If we are going to truly seek the Lord, we must "go out," as did Moses and the others who sought the Lord. We must pitch our tent "a good distance from the camp." What camp is this? For Moses, as well as for us, it is the "camp of familiarity."

Is there inherently anything wrong or sinful with the things that are familiar? No, not in themselves, but you will remember that when Jesus told His disciples to follow Him, He called them to leave the familiar pattern of their lives for extended periods and be alone with Him (Matt. 19:27; Luke 14:33). Why? Because He knew that men, by nature, are unconsciously governed by the familiar. If He would expand us to receive the eternal, He must rescue us from the limitations of the temporal.

My Spiritual Preparation for Today

Day 12
Redeem the Time

In the morning, rising up a great while before sunrise, He went out and departed to a solitary place. And there He prayed.
—Mark 1:35

We must redeem the time: cancel hobbies, forsake television, and put away the newspaper and magazines. Those who would find God find time.

Every minute you seek God is a minute enriched with new life and new power from God. Give yourself a minimum amount of time—an hour or two each day—but do not set a limit, as the Lord may draw you to seek Him on into the night. And continue day by day, and week by week, until you have drawn near enough to God that you can hear His voice, becoming confident that He is close enough to you to hear your whisper.

This is not to say we neglect our families or that we become irresponsible as we seek God. No. God has given everyone enough time to seek Him. It is there. Having done what love would have us do for our families, we simply say no to every other voice but God's.

My Spiritual Preparation for Today

Day 13
More Than Mere Men

Therefore be imitators of God as beloved children.
Walk in love, as Christ loved us and gave Himself for
us as a fragrant offering and a sacrifice to God.
—Ephesians 5:1–2

Sadly many Christians have no higher goal, no greater aspiration, than to become "normal." Their desires are limited to measuring up to others. Without a true vision of God, we most certainly will perish spiritually! Paul rebuked the church at Corinth because they walked like "mere men" (1 Cor. 3:3). God has more for us than merely becoming better people; He wants to flood our lives with the same power that raised Christ from the dead. We must understand: God does not merely want us "normal"; He wants us Christlike.

For the Holy Spirit to facilitate God's purposes in our lives, He must redefine both our definition of reality and our priorities in life. Christlikeness must become our singular goal. If we are going to become holy, we must sever the chains and restraints—the bondage of desiring just an average life. We will choose to leave the camp of familiarity and place our tent in the presence of God.

My Spiritual Preparation for Today

Day 14
Root Your Security in Christ Alone

I have set the Lord always before me; because He is at my right hand, I will not be moved.
—Psalm 16:8

For most people our sense of reality—and hence our security—is often rooted in the familiar. Indeed, most of us pass through life umbilically tied to the protection of the familiar. Experience tells us that many good people remain in lifeless churches simply because they desire the security of familiar faces more than the truth of Christ. Even people who have been delivered from adverse situations are often drawn back into hardship. Why? Because adversity is more familiar to them. Consider that certain prisoners are repeat offenders simply because they are more accustomed to prison life than freedom. Groping blindly through life, they sought for the familiar.

How difficult it is to grow spiritually if our security is based upon the stability of outward things. Our security must come from God, not circumstances or even relationships. Our sense of reality needs to be rooted in Christ. When it is, the other areas of our lives experience eternal security.

My Spiritual Preparation for Today

Day 15
Leave the Familiar

Therefore Jesus also, that He might sanctify the people
through His own blood, suffered outside the gate.
So, let us go out to Him outside the camp, bearing
His reproach. For here we do not have a lasting city,
but we are seeking the city which is to come.
—Hebrews 13:12–14, NASB

HUMANS ARE INSULATED against change by the familiar. When we work all day only to come home, watch television, then collapse in bed, our lifestyle becomes a chain of bondage. These things may not necessarily trap us in sin as much as they keep us from God.

In the same way that Moses and Jesus went outside the camp, so also must we at times leave the camp of what seems normal and predictable and begin to seek after God. This is one reason why Jesus said, "When you pray, go into your inner room, close your door and pray" (Matt. 6:6, NASB). Christ desires us to leave the familiar, distracting world of our senses and abide in the world of our hearts, bearing in mind that the highest goal of prayer is to find God.

My Spiritual Preparation for Today

Day 16
The Heart of God

For God so loved the world that He gave His
only begotten Son, that whoever believes in Him
should not perish, but have eternal life.
—John 3:16

I have been seeking God, searching to know Him and the depth of His love toward His people. I want to know Christ's heart and the compassions that motivate Him.

Mark's Gospel tells us that after Jesus taught and healed the multitudes, they became hungry. It was not enough for Him to heal and teach them; He personally cared for each of them. Their physical well-being, even concerning food, was important to Him.

So, if my quest is to know Jesus, I must recognize this about Him: Jesus loves people—all people, especially those society ignores. Therefore I must know exactly how far He would travel for men. Indeed, I must know His thoughts concerning illness, poverty, and human suffering. If I would actually do His will, I must truly know His heart. Therefore, in all my study and times of prayer I am seeking more than just knowledge; I am searching for the heart of God.

My Spiritual Preparation for Today

Day 17

JESUS POURED HIMSELF OUT

But He emptied Himself, taking upon Himself the form of a servant, and was made in the likeness of men.
—PHILIPPIANS 2:7

A LAD WITH FIVE loaves and two fish once provided food enough for Jesus to work a miracle, to feed thousands, but this miracle had to come through Christ's willing but bone-weary body. Christ had brought His disciples out that day to rest (Mark 6:31). Jesus Himself personally had come to pray and be strengthened, for John the Baptist, Jesus's forerunner, had been beheaded earlier that very week at the hands of Herod. It was in the state of being emotionally and physically depleted that Jesus fed the multitudes—not just once or twice but over and over again (v. 41, NASB). *Thousands* of men, women, and children all "ate and were satisfied" (v. 42, NASB).

Oh, the heart of Jesus! The miracle was for them, but we read of no miracle sustaining Him except the marvelous wonder of a holy love that continually lifted His tired hands with more bread and more fish. Out of increasing weakness, He repeatedly gave that others might be renewed.

MY SPIRITUAL PREPARATION FOR TODAY

Day 18
ASCEND THE HILL

Who may ascend the hill of the LORD? Who may stand in His holy place? He who has clean hands and a pure heart; who has not lifted up his soul unto vanity, nor sworn deceitfully.
—PSALM 24:3–4

AS I DRAW closer to the heart of God, the very fire of His presence begins a deep, purging work within me. In the vastness of His riches, my poverty appears.

We cannot even find the hill of the Lord, much less ascend it, if there is deceit in our hearts. How does one serve in God's holy place if his soul is unclean? It is only the pure in heart who perceive God. To ascend toward God is to walk into a furnace of truth where falsehood is extracted from our souls. To abide in the holy place, we must dwell in honesty, even when a lie might seem to save us. Each ascending step upon the hill of God is a thrusting of our souls into greater transparency, a more perfect view into the motives of our hearts.

MY SPIRITUAL PREPARATION FOR TODAY

Day 19
Search Me and Know Me

Search me, O God, and know my heart; try me, and know my concerns, and see if there is any rebellious way in me, and lead me in the ancient way.
—Psalm 139:23–24

Have you discovered your true self, the inner person whom truth alone can free? Yes, we seek holiness, but true holiness arises as the Spirit of Truth unveils the hidden places in our hearts. Indeed, it is *truthfulness* that leads to *holiness*.

Men everywhere presume to know the "truth," but they have neither holiness nor power in their lives. We are shrouded in ignorance. Barely do we know our world around us; even less do we know the nature of our own souls. Without realizing it, as we search for God's heart, we are also searching for our own. In truth, it is only in finding Him that we discover ourselves, for we are "in Him."

Truth is knowing God's heart as it was revealed in Christ, and it is knowing our own hearts in the light of God's grace. God, grant us a zeal for truth that we may stand in Your holy place!

My Spiritual Preparation for Today

Day 20

Truth Shows Our Internal Flaws

The heart is more deceitful than all things and desperately wicked; who can understand it?
—Jeremiah 17:9

I know God has created us eternally complete and perfect in Christ. I believe that. But in John's Revelation, Jesus did not tell the churches they were "perfect in His eyes." No! He revealed to them their true conditions; He told them their sins. Without compromise He placed on them the demand to be overcomers, each in their own unique and difficult circumstance.

Like them, we must know our need. And like them, the souls we want saved dwell here, in a world system structured by lies, illusions, and rampant corruption. Our old natures are like well-worn shoes in which we relax; we can be in the flesh instantly without even realizing it. For instance, are we aware of the fears and apprehensions that unconsciously influence so many of our decisions?

Thus the Holy Spirit must expose our foes before we can conquer them.

My Spiritual Preparation for Today

Day 21
Renounce Falsehood

Therefore repent and be converted, that your sins may be wiped away, that times of refreshing may come from the presence of the Lord.
—Acts 3:19

Outwardly, though we know our camera pose, do we know how we appear when we are laughing or crying, eating or sleeping, talking or angry? The fact is, most of us are ignorant of how we appear outwardly to others; much less do we know ourselves inwardly before God! Our fallen thinking processes automatically justify our actions and rationalize our thoughts. Without the Holy Spirit, we are nearly defenseless against our own innate tendencies toward self-deception.

Therefore, if we would be holy, we must first renounce falsehood. In the light of God's grace, having been justified by faith and washed in the sacrificial blood of Jesus, we need not pretend to be righteous. We need only to become truthful.

No condemnation awaits our honesty of heart—no punishment. We have only to repent and confess our sins to have them forgiven and cleansed; if we will love the truth, we shall be delivered from sin and self-deception. Indeed, we need to know two things and two things only: the heart of God in Christ and our own hearts in Christ's light.

My Spiritual Preparation for Today

Day 22

The Revelation of Christ

But we all, seeing the glory of the Lord with unveiled faces, as in a mirror, are being transformed into the same image from glory to glory by the Spirit of the Lord.
—2 Corinthians 3:18

As much as we tell others we desire close fellowship with Jesus, most of us might secretly add, "But not too close, nor too often." When the living Christ draws near, it is common to be overwhelmed by sinfulness. In the light of His purity, there is something in each of us that cries out as Peter did: "Depart from me, for I am a sinful man, O Lord!" (Luke 5:8).

At the same time, in spite of being overwhelmed by our sinfulness, the perversity of our sin nature then quickly exalts itself with our new knowledge (1 Cor. 8:1; 2 Cor. 12:7)! Barely do we glimpse the truth before we are boasting to others of what we now know, as though knowing a truth were the same as living it.

But the Holy Spirit reveals Christ because what we behold, we are to become. For as we behold the glory of the Lord, it is mirrored onto our hearts, and, in Paul's words, we are "transformed into the same image" (2 Cor. 3:18).

My Spiritual Preparation for Today

Day 23
The Lord in His Fullness

He who has My commandments and keeps them is the one who loves Me. And he who loves Me will be loved by My Father. And I will love him and will reveal Myself to him.
—John 14:21

As you mature in the Lord, a time will come when Christ will begin to reveal Himself to you as He is. Such encounters with the Living One are often alarming and full of dread. Do not be misled by the so-called religious experiences published by man, where flowers and baby angels gently unveil a docile shepherd from Heaven. *We are seeking the God of the Scriptures!* Every man who truly met the Lord Jesus Christ was filled with fear and great trembling. Nowhere in the Bible do we see anyone who was not "as a dead man" before the glorified Lord (Job 42; Isa. 6; Ezek. 1; Rev. 1). When we speak of a visitation with Christ, it is an awe-full thing of which we speak.

Yet it is for this very encounter with Jesus that the Spirit prepares us. In spite of our weaknesses and sins, God has set before us an opportunity to dwell with Him in His fullness. It is to this end that the grace of God is working in our lives.

My Spiritual Preparation for Today

Day 24
Dwell in the House of the Lord

How lovely is Your dwelling place, O Lord of Hosts!
—Psalm 84:1

Let us see that what the Promised Land was to the Israelites, Jesus Christ and the kingdom of God are to us. The Jews were called not only to know about the Promised Land but also to dwell in it and make it their home. So also are we called to dwell in Christ, where God in His kingdom becomes our abiding place.

The Hebrews had a sustaining hope during their wilderness sojourning, yet the promise of God, by itself, did not enable them to possess their inheritance. A generation watched their parents die because they complained and murmured against the Lord. Only those who learned obedience to the ways and commands of God actually *entered* and possessed their inheritance. Likewise, until we truly possess Jesus Christ—dwelling where He dwells and being trained in the ways of His kingdom—our Christianity is often an experience with hardship and frustration.

My Spiritual Preparation for Today

Day 25
Narrow Way

Because small is the gate and narrow is the way which leads to life, and there are few who find it.
—Matthew 7:14

In this time, though many are called, only a few are chosen. Why are there so few who enter, who are chosen? Because the exodus from the mind to the heart demands we become honest with ourselves. We must face and conquer the giants of sin, condemnation, and ignorance. And as it is with any journey to a distant land, the price to actually travel to that country, to taste its water and breathe its air, far exceeds the price of merely reading of its beauty in a book. Additionally we must realize that the voice of the majority, being afraid of both the battle and the cost, will be a voice of discouragement to anyone who is serious about fulfilling the promises of God. Therefore we must heed carefully the warning of Jesus that few find the narrow way that leads to life.

My Spiritual Preparation for Today

Day 26

The Balance of Truth and Grace

Grace and truth came through Jesus Christ.
—John 1:17

As the kingdom of God opens before our souls, it always seems more than we can bear and beyond our means to attain it. Such is truth to our perception.

If you hear a teaching and feel as though it were unattainable in your condition, you have only heard half the message. You missed the grace that is always resident in the heart of God's truth. Truth without grace is only half true. Truth does not stand alone in the kingdom of God. The height of God's truth is always balanced by the depth of His grace.

Remember this always: grace and truth are realized through Jesus (John 1:17). What God's truth demands, His grace will provide. Although the Holy Spirit's purpose is to "guide [us] into all the truth" (John 16:13, NASB), it is grace that supports our every step.

My Spiritual Preparation for Today

Day 27
Entering the Kingdom

Truly, truly I say to you, unless a man is born again, he cannot see the kingdom of God.... Truly, truly I say to you, unless a man is born of water and the Spirit, he cannot enter the kingdom of God.
—John 3:3, 5

God reveals Himself progressively. When we are first saved, we "see" the kingdom from a distance. We know we are going to Heaven when we die. Yet Jesus told Nicodemus that not only would he "see the kingdom of God," but also those born of water and the Spirit would "enter into the kingdom" (John 3:3–5). Our salvation begins with *seeing* the kingdom and expands to *entering* it.

To possess the kingdom, therefore, requires attitudes that are uncommon to most Christians. We must not allow ourselves the false comfort that comes with a new layer of religious information. Let us grasp that the revelation of Christ, once seen, is the swinging open of a door God calls us to enter.

My Spiritual Preparation for Today

Day 28
All the Truth

[That you may come] to know [practically, through personal experience] the love of Christ which far surpasses [mere] knowledge [without experience], that you may be filled up [throughout your being] to all the fullness of God [so that you may have the richest experience of God's presence in your lives, completely filled and flooded with God Himself].

—Ephesians 3:19, AMP

Let us open our eyes to the standard of truth that rises before us. The ancient Greeks had no word for "reality." To them, "truth" and "reality," in essence, were the same. Indeed, the Holy Spirit's purpose is to lead us into "all the truth" (John 16:13, NASB)—that is, the fullness of the reality of God.

But the reality of God is staggering! Peter did not succumb under the convicting power of "religious knowledge"—he met the reality of Jesus Christ! On the road to Damascus, Paul was not blinded and devastated by a "new doctrine"—he met the reality of Jesus Christ! It is in this explosive revelation of the Eternal that what is temporal within us finally, truly begins to believe. It is for this confrontation with Christ Himself that we need to understand the grace of God.

My Spiritual Preparation for Today

Day 29

THE MEANS TO THE END: GRACE

Fix your hope completely on the grace to be brought to you at the revelation of Jesus Christ.
—1 PETER 1:13, NASB

EVERY TIME THE Lord is revealed, two things occur: we see truth (the reality and purity of God) more fully than we dreamed possible, and we see our need of grace more assuredly than before.

Our minds must be fixed upon grace; otherwise we will always be overwhelmed and withdrawn from the presence of God. We must remind ourselves of God's great mercy and His faithfulness toward us lest we shrink from Him when He commands that we draw near.

In all things let us fix our hope upon the grace of God. As we stand in the blaze of His glory, let us remember that the nature of God is love. Let us rejoice that we belong to Jesus. He personally receives us to Himself, not as perfect beings but as those whom He seeks to free. From His view we are His promised land! Our iniquities, which have humbled us, shall not "humble" Him. Our sins are the giants He has come to defeat, enabling us to become His place of rest, His inheritance in man.

MY SPIRITUAL PREPARATION FOR TODAY

Day 30
To Know Christ

That Christ may dwell in your hearts through faith; that you, being rooted and grounded in love, may be able to comprehend with all saints what is the breadth and length and depth and height, and to know the love of Christ which surpasses all knowledge.
—Ephesians 3:17–19

If we are ever going to attain God's ultimate purpose for our lives, which is the revelation of Christ in us in glory, we are going to have to make it through each successive stage of revelation, each uncovering of His life to us and our lives to Him. We are going to see the truth of Christ and the lie of our old selves, and instead of being overwhelmed, we will stand in faith knowing the grace of God is upon us. Instead of shuddering and withdrawing when Christ appears, we will know from experience to fix our minds on the grace that accompanies His revelation. We will have learned the secret that what God's truth demands, His grace will supply.

My Spiritual Preparation for Today

Day 31

WALLS THAT KEEP US APART

I acknowledged my sin to You, and my iniquity I did not hide; I said, "I will confess my transgressions to the LORD"; and You forgave the guilt of my sin.
—PSALM 32:5, NASB

HAVE YOU EVER had a close friend but talked critically about him to someone else? The next time you were together, did you notice something almost artificial about your relationship? You were not as open or as honest with him. Because of your sin, there was a small but measurable distance between both of you. Unless there is repentance, the distance between you will probably widen until the relationship itself is over.

In the same manner that human relationships are sustained by openness and honesty, so it is also with our relationship with God. When we sin against Him, we unconsciously erect a barrier between Heaven and ourselves. Each of those defenses we have erected to keep God out ultimately walls us in, spiritually imprisoning us in our sins. Without repentance, this doesn't change.

MY SPIRITUAL PREPARATION FOR TODAY

Day 32
Remember No More

Their sins and lawless deeds will I remember no more.
—Hebrews 10:17

The love of God is such that He loves us enough to release us not only from our sin but also from the negative effects our sin has had upon our fellowship with Him. Mercifully He promises that He will not remember our sin and transgressions. Every time we ask for forgiveness, our relationship with Him becomes free and new again.

In one sweeping act of forgiveness—so complete that He promises to not even remember what we did wrong—God has provided the eternal payment for each sin we contritely ask Him to forgive. He loves us so much that, while He continues to perfect our attitudes of heart, He also provides a means to keep our relationship with Him genuine and without barriers.

My Spiritual Preparation for Today

Day 33
Redeemer

You, being dead in your sins and the uncircumcision of your flesh, He has resurrected together with Him, having forgiven you all sins. He blotted out the handwriting of ordinances that was against us and contrary to us, and He took it out of the way, nailing it to the cross.
—Colossians 2:13–14

In Christ's blood we have redemption (Eph. 1:7–8). Redemption is the "payment of a debt or obligation." There were notes, warrants held against us. We are all debtors to God, but by His death on the cross Jesus satisfied the warrants held against us.

The moment you accepted Jesus into your heart, all the things you ever did wrong—every evil thought, every angry word, and every wicked deed, each of which deserved its own punishment—were stamped REDEEMED: PAID IN FULL by our Father in Heaven. Jesus paid for them all with His blood. He is our Redeemer. He paid the price not just for the sins we previously committed but for every sin that we sincerely ask forgiveness for now. All our sins are forever forgiven and forgotten.

My Spiritual Preparation for Today

Day 34
Forgiven Forever

For it was the Father's good pleasure for all the fullness to dwell in Him, and through Him to reconcile all things to Himself, having made peace through the blood of His cross.... And although you were formerly alienated and hostile in mind, engaged in evil deeds, yet He has now reconciled you in His fleshly body through death, in order to present you before Him holy and blameless and beyond reproach.
—Colossians 1:19–22, NASB

As far as the sin issue is concerned, we must grasp the completed work of Christ. From God's eternal perspective, we are freed from sin. It is here in the realm of time, and specifically in our minds, where sin still has a temporary hold. In His great love, however, God is removing even the barriers our sins have created between Him and us.

It is important to state here that God has not lowered His standard of holiness. However, He knows we will never become holy if we are afraid to draw near to Him, for He alone is holy! Consequently He has forgiven *and* reconciled us to Himself through Jesus. The blood sacrifice of Christ has satisfied the debts of every soul who, through repentance and faith in Jesus, sincerely seeks fellowship with God.

My Spiritual Preparation for Today

Day 35
"I Don't Remember"

I, even I, am He who blots out your transgressions
for My own sake, and will not remember your sins.
—Isaiah 43:25

How many times will God forgive you? If you have truly set your heart to follow Him, He will cancel your sins as often as you ask. Will He forgive you of the worst sin you can think of? Yes! You may have to live with the consequences of your misdeed, but the redemptive power of God is such that, even in your sin, there are many things of value to be reclaimed. As for the sin itself, if you deeply and sincerely repent of it, not only will God forgive you, but He also will blot it out of His memory.

Although we often ask for cleansing, sometimes we still cannot believe the depth of God's forgiveness. But Christ placed our sin in the sea of His forgetfulness. He removed it "as far as the east is from the west" (Ps. 103:12).

My Spiritual Preparation for Today

Day 36
The Glory of the Lord

Now when Solomon had finished praying, fire came
down from heaven and consumed the burnt offering
and the sacrifices, and the glory of the Lord filled the
house. The priests could not enter into the house of the
Lord because the glory of the Lord filled the Lord's
house. All the sons of Israel, seeing the fire come down
and the glory of the Lord upon the house, bowed
down on the pavement with their faces to the ground,
and they worshiped and gave praise to the Lord.
—2 Chronicles 7:1–3, NASB

What an unparalleled event in the history of man! After Solomon dedicated the temple, the glory of the Lord descended and filled His house. What was this glory? It was the light, the bursting forth into man's world, of the radiant holiness of God Eternal. It signified that the Lord's actual person had drawn near. So great was this appearance of glory that the priests could not enter the temple.

My Spiritual Preparation for Today

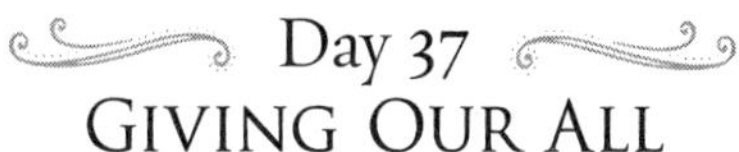

Day 37
Giving Our All

Then the king and all the people were making sacrifices before the Lord. King Solomon sacrificed twenty-two thousand oxen and one hundred and twenty thousand sheep.
—2 Chronicles 7:4–5

Consider this: the king offered 22,000 oxen and 120,000 sheep after the glory of the Lord filled the temple. They were not serving an invisible God by faith—they were in the manifested presence of the Creator Himself! Solomon could have offered one million oxen, yet it would not have satisfied the demands of his eyes as he beheld the glory of God! It is only our fathomless ignorance of who the Lord truly is that suggests a limit on any sacrifice we bring Him.

As Solomon's offering reveals, the more we see God as He is, the more compelled we are to give Him our all.

My Spiritual Preparation for Today

Day 38

Let His Glory Overcome You

Then the cloud covered the tent of meeting, and the glory of the Lord filled the tabernacle. Moses was not able to enter into the tent of meeting because the cloud settled on it, and the glory of the Lord filled the tabernacle.
—Exodus 40:34–35

Though most know of God intellectually, few know Him in His glory. Our churches tend to be sanctuaries of formality, not of the Divine Presence.

If we are part of that sector of Christianity that has rejected ritualism, in its place we simply offer varying degrees of informality. But where is God? Where is His creative, unlimited power in our gatherings? When was the last time our pastors could not stand to minister because the glory of God overwhelmed them? Such was the revelation of God in the Old Testament.

My Spiritual Preparation for Today

Day 39
THE UTTER HOLINESS OF GOD

Therefore, brethren, since we have confidence to enter the holy place by the blood of Jesus, by a new and living way which He inaugurated for us through the veil, that is, His flesh, and since we have a great priest over the house of God, let us draw near with a sincere heart in full assurance of faith.
—Hebrews 10:19–22, NASB

Ultimately the relationship between God and the Hebrews was not one of fellowship; it was almost strictly a matter of proper ritual and obedience to the law. For the Hebrews, only the high priest entered the holy place and then just once a year on the Day of Atonement. What we perceive in the carefulness of the high priest characterizes the attitude of the Old Testament Jew: no one dared approach the holy, living presence of God without perfectly fulfilling the law. Eventually the Jews stopped writing and speaking the sacred name of God. Even His name was too holy to be uttered in this world.

As Christians, through the blood of Jesus, God has opened the way for us to enter the holy place of His presence. God is holy, but now we have a way to reach Him.

My Spiritual Preparation for Today

Day 40
Grace and Holiness, Together

Our old man has been crucified with Him, so that the body of sin might be destroyed, and we should no longer be slaves to sin. For the one who has died is freed from sin.
—Romans 6:6–7

This very sense of God's holiness is one of the main reasons why the first-century church in Jerusalem was so powerful. As Jews, they knew the holiness of God's law. But as Christians, they possessed the knowledge of His grace; they knew personally the Lamb, the perfect sacrifice, who had come and fulfilled the requirements of the law. God, even He whom the Jews worshipped, had taken human form and given *Himself* for sin!

Many Christians the world over celebrate the forgiveness of sins in Christ, but they end their experience with God there. Jews, who knew historically the fearful justice of God, still lived outside the Divine Presence because they did not understand the forgiveness of sins in Christ. But it is the union of both truths that produces power in our lives and leads us into the reality of God.

My Spiritual Preparation for Today

Day 41
Escape to Forgiveness

Let us then come with confidence to the throne of grace, that we may obtain mercy and find grace to help in time of need.
—Hebrews 4:16

There are many times when we feel unworthy, when we seek to escape from the person of God. In these times the last one we want to face is God in His holiness. But in the midst of our unworthiness, let us call upon the Lord. We can escape *to* God for forgiveness.

When John the Baptist looked at Jesus, he told his disciples, "Behold, the Lamb of God who takes away the sin of the world!" (John 1:29, NASB). The Lamb of God has taken away not just the sins of the world but *your* sins as well. Christ's sacrifice is much more than all the bulls and sheep ever offered throughout all of time; He perfectly satisfies the demand of God's holy justice. And while the high priest drew near with fear and terror, we can draw near with confidence through the blood of Christ—so great and complete is the sacrifice God has provided!

My Spiritual Preparation for Today

Day 42
THE LAW OF LIBERTY

So speak and so do as those who will be judged by the law of liberty. For he who has shown mercy will have judgment without mercy, for mercy triumphs over judgment.
—JAMES 2:12–13

THE JUSTICE OF God's law is holy, but the sacrifice of the Son of God is holier still, for "mercy triumphs over judgment" (James 2:13). The Lord who filled Solomon's temple with His presence will fill, *and is filling,* His people today. We have the inexhaustible sacrifice Himself seated upon the throne of grace—it is He who is calling us to boldly come before Him. Enter, therefore, into His glory by the blood of the Lamb. Let Jesus wash your heart of its sins. For our goal is to live in the presence of the very same holy God who appeared in His glory to the Hebrews!

MY SPIRITUAL PREPARATION FOR TODAY

Day 43
THE SHELTER OF GOD

He raised us up and seated us together in the heavenly places in Christ Jesus, so that in the coming ages He might show the surpassing riches of His grace in kindness toward us in Christ Jesus.
—EPHESIANS 2:6–7

TO FIND THE shelter of God, we must stand with the Lord against sin and compromise. These things must be destroyed or they will destroy us. The transformation of our souls positions us outside the devil's reach. It raises us up spiritually to seat us in heavenly places.

It is one thing to know doctrinally that we are positioned with Christ in Heaven; it is quite another thing to spiritually function in that lofty place. (See Ephesians 1:20; 2:6.) To motivate us toward Christlikeness, the Holy Spirit not only instructs us in doctrinal truths, but He also thrusts us into storms of conflict and satanic assault. It is in the midst of this confrontation with hell that He works in us the virtues of Heaven.

MY SPIRITUAL PREPARATION FOR TODAY

Day 44
Tempted and Tried

Then Jesus was led up into the wilderness by the Spirit to be tempted by the devil.
—Matthew 4:1

Our walk with God progresses from learning lessons to having what we just learned tested. This was the Father's pattern with His Son, and it is His pattern with us as well. Let us, therefore, consider Jesus. Just after Christ was baptized by John, the Father affirmed His sonship. What was the next scene? Jesus was compelled by the Holy Spirit into the wilderness.

When we think about being "Spirit led," we envision miracles, healings, and winning the multitudes. But before Jesus was led to do wonders, He was led to do battle; and the war was over the purity of His heart. Jesus was led to the wilderness to be tempted (Matt. 4:1). As much as the Father loved His Son, as perfectly as He knew Him, yet still the Father proved the character of His Son through conflict.

My Spiritual Preparation for Today

Day 45
Proven in Adversity

No temptation has taken you except what is common to man. God is faithful, and He will not permit you to be tempted above what you can endure, but will with the temptation also make a way to escape, that you may be able to bear it.
—1 Corinthians 10:13

The word *tempted* actually means "tested or proven in adversity." Jesus Himself was always without sin, yet He learned obedience through the things He suffered and His temptation in the wilderness. Likewise, the Father is not hesitant about allowing the enemy a measured assault against us. He is not worried that we will break. In fact, He desires a certain degree of brokenness before He can use us.

My Spiritual Preparation for Today

Day 46
Let the Storms Come

Beloved, do not be surprised at the fiery ordeal among you, which comes upon you for your testing, as though some strange thing were happening to you; but to the degree that you share the sufferings of Christ, keep on rejoicing, so that also at the revelation of His glory you may rejoice with exultation.
—1 Peter 4:12–13, NASB

Life consists of learning lessons and passing tests. The integrity of God requires that our learning not be mere head knowledge but that our hearts be conformed to Christ. Indeed, before the Lord is through with us, the way of Christ will be more than something we know; it will be something we instinctively choose in the midst of temptation or battle. This is where we graduate into the power of God.

So let the storms come. Do not fear the threat of life's fire. God has promised to be with us in our adversity. It is there we attain greater purity.

My Spiritual Preparation for Today

Day 47

Jesus's Holiness

I need to be baptized by You, and do You come to me?
—Matthew 3:14

John the Baptist was filled with the Holy Spirit "while yet in his mother's womb" (Luke 1:15, NASB). Only Jesus knew the fallen condition of the human heart more perfectly than John. In fact, Jesus testified that John was "more than a prophet." John was a "seer prophet," which meant he had open vision into the spirit realm. John had insight into the secrets of men's hearts. Understand this about prophets: they are aware of things that are hidden from other men.

But when Jesus came to be baptized, *before* the heavens opened and the Holy Spirit descended, John saw something that was overwhelming even to his standard of righteousness. He gazed into Jesus's heart, and he saw *no sins, no lies, no lusts*. John saw a level of holiness that, without knowing he was gazing at the Messiah, caused him to utter with astonishment, "I need to be baptized by You" (Matt. 3:14).

My Spiritual Preparation for Today

Day 48
"I Have Need!"

The next day John saw Jesus coming toward him and said, "Look, the Lamb of God, who takes away the sin of the world."
—John 1:29

Jesus, as the Lamb of God, was without spot or blemish. This is exactly what the prophet beheld in Jesus: spotless purity of heart. Christ's virtue took John's breath away! The powerful emanation of Christ's inner purity made John immediately aware of his own need. When John saw Jesus, he discovered a level of righteousness that was higher, purer than his own. This great prophet looked into the heart of Jesus, and in the brightness of Christ's holiness he cried, "I have need."

And so it is with us. Each time we see Jesus, each successive revelation of Christ's purity makes our need more apparent. As Christ's holiness unfolds before us, we cannot but echo the same cry of John the Baptist: "I have need to be baptized by You!" (Matt. 3:14, NASB).

My Spiritual Preparation for Today

Day 49
God's Answer to Our Need

Therefore Jesus also, so that He might sanctify the people with His own blood, suffered outside the gate.
—Hebrews 13:12

In the beginning of our walk, we embraced life in our own strength, trusting in our own skills for success and attainment. Yes, we turned to God, but mainly in times of grief or trial. But as the Lord brings us into maturity, what we once considered strengths are actually discovered to be more subtle and, therefore, more dangerous weaknesses. Our pride and self-confidence keep us from God's help; the clamor of our many ideas and desires drown the whisper of the still, small voice of God. Indeed, in God's eyes, the best of human successes are still "wretched and miserable and poor and blind and naked" (Rev. 3:17, NASB).

In time, we discover that all true strength, all true effectiveness—yes, our very holiness itself—begins with discovering our need. We grow weaker, less confident in our abilities. As the outer shell of self-righteousness crumbles, *Jesus Himself* becomes God's answer to every man who cries for holiness and power in his walk.

My Spiritual Preparation for Today

Day 50
The Power of Godliness

For God has not given us the spirit of fear, but
of power, and love, and self-control.
—2 Timothy 1:7

There is power in godliness. Jesus was holy, and He was powerful. Paul was holy, and he was powerful. Peter and John were holy, and they were powerful. Beware of those who have a form of godliness but deny the power thereof. A holy life is a powerful life.

Many Christians look for shortcuts to the power of God. To try shortcuts is to become, at best, frustrated; at worst, a false teacher or prophet. Listen very carefully: there is tremendous power for us in God, but not without holiness. Holiness precedes power.

My Spiritual Preparation for Today

Day 51
Holiness Precedes Power

Since we have these promises, beloved, let us cleanse ourselves from all filthiness of the flesh and spirit, perfecting holiness in the fear of God.
—2 Corinthians 7:1

We are so eager to do something for God—anything, as long as we do not have to change inside. God does not need what we can do; He wants what we are. He wants to make us a holy people. Jesus lived thirty years of sinless purity before He did one work of power! His goal was not to do some great work but to please the Father with a holy life.

Hear me: our goal, likewise, is not to become powerful but to become holy with Christ's presence. God promises to empower that which He first makes holy. Do you want your Christianity to work? Then seek Jesus Himself as your source and standard of holiness. Do you want to see the power of God in your life? Then seek to know Christ's purity of heart. If we are becoming the people Jesus calls His own, we should be growing in holiness. A mature Christian will be both holy and powerful, but holiness will precede power.

My Spiritual Preparation for Today

Day 52
Keep Pure

How can a young man keep his way pure? By keeping it according to Your word. With all my heart I have sought You; do not let me wander from Your commandments. Your word I have treasured in my heart, that I may not sin against You.
—Psalm 119:9–11, NASB

The question is not, "How can a young man become pure?" as though purity of heart is impossible for a young man. Rather, the question is, "How can he *keep* his way pure?" Purity of heart can be reached and maintained if we abide in fellowship with God's Word. There is a place beyond knowing a few Bible verses, a place where the living Word of God becomes our most treasured possession.

To treasure the Word is to remain fully vulnerable, even as it judges "the thoughts and intents of the heart" (Heb. 4:12). It exposes our motives. It illuminates the darkness of our hearts with light. It sets us free from the strongholds of hidden sin. It wounds, but it also heals. The Word of the Lord, united with the Holy Spirit, is the vehicle of our transformation into the image of Christ. Holiness comes to him whose treasure is the Word.

My Spiritual Preparation for Today

Day 53

Treasure Every Word

For as many of you as have been baptized
into Christ have put on Christ.
—Galatians 3:27

Many read the Scriptures simply to reinforce their current beliefs. Although they read the entire Bible, their mind only sees certain doctrines. Instead of believing what they read, they merely read what they already believe. Christians are often baptized into their denomination. When they are fully indoctrinated, their minds have been immersed into a pool of teaching that leaves them more conformed to the image of their sect than to the likeness of Christ.

But if we would grow in Christ's likeness, we must be baptized into Christ's Spirit, not the spirit or slant of any particular denomination. When one is baptized in Christ, his spirit is actually clothed with Christ. It is Christ's image in holiness and power that a true disciple seeks. We cannot allow ourselves to be inoculated with a dozen or so special Bible verses that merely get us "saved" but leave us immune from the fullness of God. You are a disciple of Jesus Christ: the reality of God's kingdom is found in the combined meaning of all Jesus taught. Therefore you must treasure every word!

My Spiritual Preparation for Today

Day 54
The Spirit in the Word

Therefore, putting aside all filthiness and all that remains of wickedness, in humility receive the word implanted, which is able to save your souls.
—James 1:21, NASB

The Word is God. The Scriptures are not God, but the Spirit that breathes through the words is God. And this Holy Spirit should be honored as God. Therefore, as you seek the Lord, place your Bible at the foot of your bed and kneel as you read; are you not seeking to meet with the Almighty? Pray that you will not merely read intellectually. Rather, ask the Holy Spirit to speak to your heart through the Word.

To be a true disciple, you must tremble when God speaks (Isa. 66:2). Prepare your heart with reverence and worship. As you kneel in humility before the Lord, the Word will be engrafted into your soul, actually becoming a part of your nature (James 1:21). Be prepared to take notes, to write down what the Spirit says, being ever mindful that it is the quickening Spirit, not the letter, that brings life (2 Cor. 3:6).

My Spiritual Preparation for Today

Day 55
THE PIERCING OF THE WORD

For the Word of God is alive, and active, and sharper than any two-edged sword, piercing even to the division of soul and spirit, of joints and marrow, and able to judge the thoughts and intents of the heart.
—HEBREWS 4:12

AS YOU READ Scripture, read with an attitude of willingness, humility, and repentance, and even if you cannot fully obey the Word, hold it in your heart. This is where most people fall short. If the command seems impossible or unreasonable to their minds, they disregard it. But Jesus said, "He who has My commandments and keeps them is the one who loves Me" (John 14:21). Many times, before you are able to obey the Word, you must make yourself keep it. God must work in you "both to will and to work" (Phil. 2:13, NASB). First God makes you willing, and then He makes you able.

Let the Word pierce you; let it crucify you. Suffer with it, but do not let it go. View every Bible command, every "Thou shalt be," as a promise God will fulfill in your life as you steadfastly keep His Word. And as you keep the Word, treasuring His commandments in your heart, the Word itself will effectually work within you, bringing grace and transformation as you believe.

MY SPIRITUAL PREPARATION FOR TODAY

Day 56
Hide the Word

Your word I have hidden in my heart,
that I might not sin against You.
—Psalm 119:11

Each of us needs to stockpile in our minds as much of the Bible as we can. During the first ten years of my walk with God, each day I read five chapters in the Pentateuch (the first five books of the Bible). I would then read aloud five psalms, carefully study one chapter of Proverbs and three chapters in the Prophets, read three chapters in one of the New Testament Epistles, and read one chapter in the Gospels. When the Spirit spoke to me, I honored Him by following His leading, being careful to write down all that He taught. The next day I would begin my pattern again by kneeling before the Word.

Whatever approach you decide upon, combine Old and New Testaments in your pursuit. This will keep you balanced in the various truths of the Bible. Keep the pattern diligently until the Holy Spirit begins to speak or "breathe" through the Scriptures. We are called to *abide* in Him, not just visit with Him. You can do this through diligently studying the Word.

My Spiritual Preparation for Today

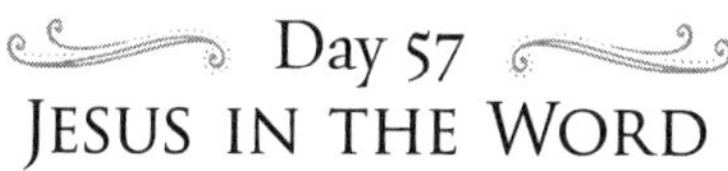

Day 57
Jesus in the Word

Let the word of Christ dwell in you richly.
—Colossians 3:16

We must be fully given to the words of Jesus. The Gospels must rise to preeminence above all other books in the Bible. Too often Christians preach Paul or another one of the apostles more than Jesus. It was the word of Christ that transformed all the apostles. The apostle John taught, "Anyone who goes too far and does not abide in the teaching of Christ, does not have God" (2 John 9, NASB).

We are called to abide in the teaching of Christ. Yet, typically, Christians have spent little time in Christ's words, choosing rather to read about Him than dwell within Him. Dear ones, truth is in Jesus (Eph. 4:21). Therefore, we must learn to abide in the teaching of Christ, even while we pursue our study of the rest of the Scriptures. Only Jesus died for our sins; our pursuit of *Him* must become the singular goal of our spiritual endeavors.

My Spiritual Preparation for Today

Day 58

The Word and Temptation

In the beginning was the Word, and the Word was with God, and the Word was God.... Yet to all who received Him, He gave the power to become sons of God, to those who believed in His name, who were born not of blood, nor of the will of the flesh, nor of the will of man, but of God.
—John 1:1, 12–13

The Scriptures tell us that the Lord is our keeper. To be kept by Him, however, does not mean we will not face temptations, for even Jesus was tempted. Rather, it is in the midst of trials and temptations that God keeps us. And the way He keeps us is through His Word. Therefore, if we would be holy, we must know intimately the Person whom the Bible calls the Word.

You must develop such a listening ear that the Spirit could speak to you anywhere about anything. Honor Him, and He will honor you. Keep the Word in your heart, and He will establish you in holiness before God. He will keep your way pure.

My Spiritual Preparation for Today

Day 59
Becoming Holy

You desire truth in the inward parts, and in the hidden part You make me to know wisdom. Purify me with hyssop, and I will be clean; wash me, and I will be whiter than snow.
—Psalm 51:6–7

Sin wears a cloak of deception. Therefore, the first stage of attaining holiness involves the exposure of our hearts to truth and the cleansing of our hearts from lies. This process of becoming holy is accomplished by the Holy Spirit, and the way the Spirit sanctifies us is with the truth. Once the Spirit breaks the power of deception in our lives, He can break the power of sin.

Jesus described those who bear fruit in the kingdom as having "an honest and good heart, and hold it fast [the Word], and bear fruit with perseverance" (Luke 8:15, NASB). The first virtue necessary for fruitfulness to come forth is honesty of heart. For without a love of the truth, no area of our lives can be corrected.

My Spiritual Preparation for Today

Day 60
HIDDEN SIN

Therefore, confess your sins to one another, and pray for one another so that you may be healed. The effective prayer of a righteous man can accomplish much.
—JAMES 5:16, NASB

THE BIBLE WARNS us that sin is deceitful (Heb. 3:13). Thus, we must vigilantly take "every thought into captivity to the obedience of Christ" (2 Cor. 10:5). If we would discern the voice of iniquity, we must recognize its lie when it says, "Your sin is not so bad." For sin engulfs the mind in a cloud of alibis and cover-ups as it seeks to keep itself alive. It twists and distorts the truth, and without plans for repentance it calmly reassures us, "God understands; He'll never judge me."

Should an embarrassing sin nearly be exposed through circumstances or another manner, we thank God that our secret problem remained hidden. As likely as not, however, it was not God who kept the sin hidden; it was the devil. The attitude of Heaven toward sin is plain. We are to confess our sins to one another and to renounce "the things hidden because of shame" (2 Cor. 4:2, NASB). Confession and exposure bring sin to the light. They break the power of deception.

MY SPIRITUAL PREPARATION FOR TODAY

Day 61
Enslaved to Sin

"You will know the truth, and the truth will make you free." They answered Him, "We are Abraham's descendants and have never yet been enslaved to anyone; how is it that You say, 'You will become free'?" Jesus answered them, "Truly, truly, I say to you, everyone who commits sin is the slave of sin."
—John 8:32–34, NASB

Sin is slavery. When the Lord delivered Israel from Egypt, the Hebrews celebrated their freedom with great joy. Yet inwardly they still thought very much like slaves, not free men. Similarly Christ has set us free from the tyranny of sin. We are legally free, yet to experience that freedom we must be renewed in the spirit of our minds.

My Spiritual Preparation for Today

Day 62
Love the Truth

They did not receive the love for the truth that they might be saved.
—2 Thessalonians 2:10

The Scriptures warn of those who "did not receive the love of the truth that they might be saved." (2 Thess. 2:10). Salvation is not a religious rite; it is the experience of being saved from that which would otherwise destroy us. Indeed, Jesus came to "save His people from their sins" (Matt. 1:21). The freedom that comes from knowing the truth is freedom from sin and its consequences.

For those who do not love the truth, God allows a "deluding influence" (Greek, "activity of error") to come upon them, "that they will believe what is false, in order that they all may be judged who did not believe the truth, but took pleasure in wickedness" (2 Thess. 2:11–12, NASB). Each area of your life where truth is not ruling has for its substitute an "activity of error."

My Spiritual Preparation for Today

Day 63
BREAK THE LIES

He who is often reproved, yet hardens his neck, will suddenly be destroyed, and that without remedy.
—PROVERBS 29:1

EACH TIME YOU repent of a sin, a lie that once controlled your life is broken. But if you take pleasure in wickedness, refusing God's kindness, which leads you to repentance, God eventually will give you over to the deception your rebellion has demanded. This is why Jesus taught us to pray, "Do not lead us into temptation, but deliver us from evil" (Matt. 6:13, NASB). God does not tempt man with sin. Temptation and evil both are inherent in our old natures. If we continually, stubbornly refuse to repent for a sin, God gives us over to that which we refuse to surrender.

Paul also warns of those who "exchanged the truth of God for a lie" (Rom. 1:25, NASB). Every sin is the exchange of the truth of God for a lie. Consequently, the more truthful one becomes with himself and God, the more he is delivered from sin and its deceitfulness, allowing righteousness to come forth.

MY SPIRITUAL PREPARATION FOR TODAY

Day 64
Become Blameless

No lie was found in their mouths, for they are without fault before the throne of God.
—Revelation 14:5

To become blameless is to be free from falsehood; it is to be delivered from sin and the deception that protects sin. Yet this process of deliverance is not attained if we are only casually committed to the Lord Jesus. We must be dedicated to the way of truth. Indeed, each of us has been conditioned by decades of unbelief, fear, and an unbridled thought life, which have reinforced deception.

Christians, who tend to automatically assume they are the "chosen of God," have reassured themselves that they could not possibly be deceived. The very thought "I cannot be deceived" is itself a deception! Let us stay humble and not presume that the *calling* of God and the *choosing* of God are alike. "Many are called," Jesus taught, "but few are chosen" (Matt. 22:14). Many tests await the called before they are equipped by God and become His chosen; not the least of these tests is becoming free from deception.

My Spiritual Preparation for Today

Day 65
Be Sanctified

Blessed are the pure in heart, for they shall see God.
—Matthew 5:8

Sanctification does not come automatically. We are told to pray for "the sanctification without which no one will see the Lord" (Heb. 12:14, NASB). We must pray for holiness. Without seriously pursuing sanctification, no one will see the Lord.

Jesus prayed, "[Father,] sanctify them in the truth; Your word is truth" (John 17:17, NASB). He was saying, "Father, purify them of the lies and illusions of this age through Your penetrating Word." In Ephesians, Paul tells us that Christ sanctifies the church by cleansing her "by the washing of water with the word...that she would be holy and blameless" (Eph. 5:26–27, NASB). This, then, embracing the truth and allowing the Word of Truth to do its work of sanctification, cleansing, and purification in our lives, is the process through which we become holy. Loving the truth is the beginning of our freedom from sin.

My Spiritual Preparation for Today

Day 66
The Severity of Sin

For the wages of sin is death, but the gift of God
is eternal life through Jesus Christ our Lord.
—Romans 6:23

There is a serious error in our understanding concerning sin. Certain Bible commentators have casually declared that *sin* in the Greek Scriptures is merely "missing the mark." That phrase was coined to define the broadest use of the word, but it was woefully inadequate in defining the consequences of sin. For the consequences of sin are death (Rom. 6:23).

When we examine the entire picture concerning Christ's attitude toward sin, we can see it was much worse than just a "bad shot." Indeed, in reference to sin Jesus said, "I tell you…unless you repent, you will all likewise perish" (Luke 13:3, 5). In respect to sin and the kingdom of God, He declared, "If your eye causes you to sin, pluck it out. It is better for you to enter the kingdom of God with one eye than with two eyes to be thrown into the fire of hell" (Mark 9:47).

You see, sin is not merely missing the mark; it is missing the kingdom. It is living in death when we could be living in life!

My Spiritual Preparation for Today

Day 67
Faith Held Hostage

I did not keep from declaring what was beneficial
to you, and teaching you publicly and from house to
house, testifying to both Jews and Greeks of repentance
toward God and of faith in our Lord Jesus Christ.
—Acts 20:20–21

Faith is essential to reach purity of heart, for you must first believe that holiness is possible or you will never attempt to reach it. But without repentance, faith is held hostage by the lawlessness of sin. God will not favor the faith of a sinful man unless that man is in a state of repentance. James tells us that "the effectual fervent prayer of a *righteous* man availeth much" (James 5:16, KJV, emphasis added). Repentance prepares the heart for righteousness; it unlocks the power of faith toward God.

The consequences of sin are to take us beyond simply feeling sorry we sinned. God wants to bring us into an *attitude* of repentance that persistently returns to Him until the power of faith is unlocked and the fruit of righteousness comes forth in our lives.

My Spiritual Preparation for Today

Day 68
Repentance Is the Beginning

John indeed baptized with the baptism of repentance, telling the people that they should believe in the One coming after him, that is, in Christ Jesus.
—Acts 19:4

The Bible tells us that prior to the beginning of Christ's ministry, a man named John came (John 1:6). John the Baptist was sent from God. His baptism of repentance was not the last event of the old covenant to be completed; it was the first event, *the groundbreaker,* of the new covenant. John was sent by God as a forerunner to Christ's ministry. His unique purpose was to immerse Israel into an attitude of repentance (Acts 19:4). He was called to go before Christ. His task was to "prepare" and "make ready the way of the Lord" (Mark 1:2–3, NASB).

Repentance always precedes the coming forth of the living Christ in a person's life. To "prepare" and "make ready" is the purpose of repentance. Let us be sure we understand: John's repentance did not merely make men sorry; it made men ready.

My Spiritual Preparation for Today

Day 69
The Fruit of Repentance

Therefore bear fruit in keeping with repentance.
—Matthew 3:8, nasb

True repentance is to turn over the soil of the heart for a new planting of concepts and directives. It is a vital aspect in the overall sphere of spiritual maturity. To truly change your mind takes time and effort. Just as John the Baptist commanded the Jews to "bear fruit in keeping with repentance," let us also realize that repentance is not over until fruit is brought forth. In effect, John was saying, "Cease not your turning away from pride until you delight in lowliness. Continue repenting of selfishness until love is natural to you. Do not stop mourning your impurities until you are pure." He demanded men keep with repentance until fruit was manifested. And if you will be holy, you will continue in repentance until you are holy.

My Spiritual Preparation for Today

Day 70
PERSIST

If we confess our sins, He is faithful and just to forgive us our sins and cleanse us from all unrighteousness.
—1 JOHN 1:9

AN EXHORTATION: PERSIST in your repentance, never doubting the generosity of God's mercy. If God commands us to forgive unconditionally those who sin against us (Matt. 18:21–22), know that God does not require of us more than He demands of Himself. If you sin 490 times in one day, after each time cry to Him for forgiveness. He will both forgive you and cleanse you of sin's effect. Do not hide from your sins; confess them. God's grace and the sacrifice of His Son are enough to cover and forgive any and every sin, but we must ask for forgiveness. We must humble ourselves and, from the heart, submit again to God. Be honest about your sin, and He will cleanse you of it.

MY SPIRITUAL PREPARATION FOR TODAY

Day 71

"Until I Have Perfected You"

I am confident of this very thing, that He who began a good work in you will perfect it until the day of Jesus Christ.
—Philippians 1:6

During one period in my life I repeatedly stumbled over the same problem. Grieved and doubting in my heart, I cried out, "Lord! How long will You put up with me?" In a flash of grace and truth He answered, "Until I have perfected you."

The Scriptures tell us, "Reproofs of instruction are the way of life" (Prov. 6:23, KJV). This is not burdensome except to those who refuse correction. The way of reproof *is* the way of life! Jesus said that He disciplines those He loves; therefore, we should turn to repentance (Rev. 3:19). It is not God's wrath that speaks to us of repentance; it is His loving-kindness. As long as we desire to be like Him, His rebuke will be a door into His presence.

My Spiritual Preparation for Today

Day 72

Recoiling at Repentance

I tell you, no! But unless you repent, you will all likewise perish.
—Luke 13:3

Do not despise repentance. Every season of significant spiritual growth in your walk with God will be precipitated by a time of deep repentance. If, however, you recoil at the word *repentance*, it is because you do not want to change. You need to know the importance of repentance. When the thought of repentance is not shrouded in gloomy images of sackcloth and tears, when correction inspires rejoicing and shouts of praise to God's grace, know that your spirit has truly become pure. It is at this point you are walking the way God calls holy.

My Spiritual Preparation for Today

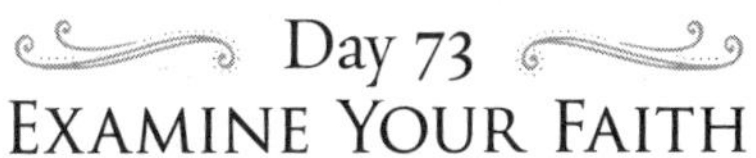

Day 73
Examine Your Faith

But examine everything carefully;
hold fast to that which is good.
—1 Thessalonians 5:21, NASB

Would you buy a car without driving it? Of course not! Yet many of us accept various "plans of salvation" that do not really save us from the distresses of hell. In spite of the fact that Jesus came to give us abundant life, we remain sick, sinful, and selfish. If our Christianity does not work in this life where we can test it, it is foolhardy to hope it will successfully transport us into eternity where, if we fail the test, we suffer eternal separation from God.

I do not wish to imply, however, that unless we get every doctrine right and every interpretation perfect, we will be refused entrance into Heaven. Christianity is more a matter of the heart than the head; it is a maturing of love more than knowledge. The test of truth is not an intellectual pursuit but whether you are drawing closer, week by week, to knowing and loving Jesus Christ.

My Spiritual Preparation for Today

Day 74
Questions for Faith

In this way God's love is perfected in us, so that we may have boldness on the Day of Judgment, because as He is, so are we in this world.
—1 John 4:17

If we have been indoctrinated to believe that the kingdom of God—and Christianity itself—does not really have to work, or if the absence of holiness and power fails to trouble us, something is wrong with our concept of truth.

In testing our faith, we should seek answers to three very important questions. First: *Is my faith effective?* Ask yourself if your prayers are being answered and if your life is becoming godly. Second: *If my doctrines do not work, then why not?* You must seek to find out why things are not working for you. And third: *If I do see the fruit and power of the Holy Spirit revealed in another's life, how did he (or she) receive such grace from God?* Do not be afraid to sit as a disciple under the anointing of another's ministry.

The final test of faith is seen in the kind of life it produces. Continual, persistent walking with Christ will produce a life like Christ's. We will walk as He did, with holiness and power.

My Spiritual Preparation for Today

Day 75
TRUSTING OUR TEACHERS

Jesus answered them, "Take heed that no one deceives you. For many will come in My name, saying, 'I am the Christ,' and will deceive many."
—MATTHEW 24:4–5

ALL TOO OFTEN, Christians accept teachings "by faith"—not faith in the living God but faith that their church doctrines are correct. We unconsciously hope that whoever is teaching us has not made a mistake.

We must recognize the fallibility of all our teachers. Remaining free from deception is a responsibility each of us must assume as individuals. Without becoming suspicious or mistrusting, in humility let us reexamine what we have been taught. The virtue of any teaching is in its ability to either equip you to do God's will or empower you to find God's heart. If either objective is missing, the information is not worth your time.

MY SPIRITUAL PREPARATION FOR TODAY

Day 76
Dead Religion

And many false prophets will rise and will deceive many.
—Matthew 24:11

Five times in Matthew 24 Jesus warned against deception in the last days (vv. 4, 5, 11, 23–24, 26). If we are not at least somewhat troubled by those warnings, it is only because we are guarding our ignorance with arrogance, presuming that our thoughts must be right simply because *we* think them. There are areas in all of our lives that need to be corrected. And unless we can be corrected, unless we are seeking God for an unfolding revelation of His Son, our so-called "faith" may be, in reality, just a lazy indifference, a deception concerning the things of God. *Subconsciously we may actually want a dead religion so we do not have to change.*

Yes, we should accept many things by faith. But faith is not blindly sticking our hand out to be led by another blind man. It is not an excuse to justify impotent doctrines. True faith is freighted with the power of God.

My Spiritual Preparation for Today

Day 77
THE POWER OF HOLINESS

Know this: In the last days perilous times will come.
Men will be lovers of themselves, lovers of money...
having a form of godliness, but denying its power.
—2 TIMOTHY 3:1–5

HOLINESS IS POWERFUL. Have you ever met a truly holy man or woman? There is a power in their godliness. If, however, one has never known a Christlike soul, it becomes very easy to fake Christianity. Remember this always: being false is natural to the human heart; it is with much effort that we become true. Unless we are reaching for spiritual maturity, our immaturity shapes our perceptions of God. We point to the Almighty and say, "He stopped requiring godliness," when, in reality, we have compromised the standards of His kingdom. *Know for certain that the moment we stop obeying God, we start faking Christianity.*

MY SPIRITUAL PREPARATION FOR TODAY

Day 78
True Knowledge of the Lord

I have been crucified with Christ. It is no longer I who live, but Christ who lives in me. And the life I now live in the flesh, I live by faith in the Son of God, who loved me and gave Himself for me.
—Galatians 2:20

The "knowledge of the Lord" is not a ten-week course to be passed; it is an unfolding experience with Jesus Christ. It starts with rebirth and faith in Jesus, but it continues on into Christ's own holiness, power, and perfection. And as we mature, we begin to realize that the Spirit of Christ is actually within us. The cross emerges off the printed page; it stands upright before us, confronting us with our own Gethsemanes, our own Golgothas—but also our own resurrections through which we ascend spiritually into the true presence of the Lord.

My Spiritual Preparation for Today

Day 79
HOLY LIVING

Not that I have already attained or have already been perfected, but I follow after it so that I may lay hold of that for which I was seized by Christ Jesus.
—PHILIPPIANS 3:12

OUR EXPERIENCE OF Christianity must go beyond just being another interpretation of the Bible; it must expand until our faith in Jesus and our love for Him become a lightning rod for His presence. We should be living holy, powerful lives. No excuses. If we are not holy or if there is not the power of godliness in our lives, let us not blame God. Let us persevere in seeking God until we find Him, until we discover "what [we are] still lacking" (Matt. 19:20, NASB). Let us press on.

How long should we continue to seek Him? If we spent all our lives and all our energies for three minutes of genuine Christlikeness, we would have spent our lives well. We do not want to just give mental assent to Christian doctrine; we want to see, have contact with, and live in the experienced reality of Christ's actual presence. The moment we settle for anything less, our Christianity starts becoming false.

MY SPIRITUAL PREPARATION FOR TODAY

Day 80
Destroy Idols

Watch yourself that you make no covenant with the inhabitants of the land into which you are going, or it will become a snare in your midst. But rather, you are to tear down their altars and smash their sacred pillars and cut down their Asherim—for you shall not worship any other god, for the Lord, whose name is Jealous, is a jealous God.
—Exodus 34:12–14, NASB

Christ does not personally destroy the idols of sin and self within us. Rather, He points to them and tells us to destroy them. This message is about repentance. If you withdraw from the sound of that word, it is because you need a fresh cleansing of your soul. In fact, we are talking about a type of repentance that is uncommon to those who only seek forgiveness but not change. We are speaking of deep repentance—a vigilant, contrite attitude that refuses to allow sin or self to become an idol in our hearts.

From the scripture above we see that Jesus does not want us to "carefully" take down that hidden altar of sin so we will not break it; rather He commands that we "tear down" what is offensive. When He shows us an inner idol, we must demolish it completely. We cannot secretly harbor the slightest intention of ever using that idol again. It must be destroyed.

My Spiritual Preparation for Today

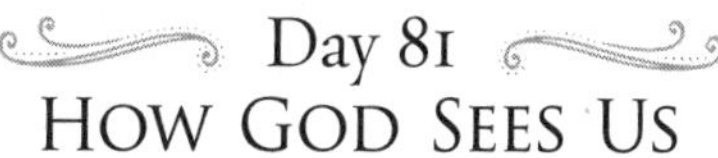

Day 81
How God Sees Us

All things were created by Him and for Him.
—Colossians 1:16

There are many aspects to the nature of Christ. He is the Good Shepherd, our deliverer, and our healer. We perceive God through the filter of our need of Him. And thus He has ordained, for He Himself is our one answer to a thousand needs.

But how does Jesus see us? Looking through His eyes, the church is His bride: bone of His bones and flesh of His flesh (Eph. 5:22–32). He has not saved us so we can live for ourselves again; He has saved us for Himself. True salvation is a betrothal. He purifies us for our marriage. From His perspective, our independent ways are idolatrous. They kindle the fires of His jealousy. An idol is not an occasional sin; it is something that rules us and makes us its slave. Whatever challenges Jesus's right to our hearts becomes His enemy, which He will confront.

My Spiritual Preparation for Today

Day 82
The Antichrist Spirit

Every spirit that does not confess that Jesus Christ has come in the flesh is not from God. This is the spirit of the antichrist, which you have heard is coming and is already in the world.
—1 John 4:3

The apostle John perceived antichrist not only as one who was coming but also as a spiritual enemy that sought to infiltrate and then replace true Christianity (1 John 2:18; 4:3). The antichrist spirit is a religious spirit; it is manifested in that thinking that refuses to be taught and corrected by Christ or anyone else. The spirit of antichrist is resident in much of the church today, opposing the move of God, displaying itself as being God.

Simply put, the spirit of antichrist is that spirit that exalts *self* as *deity*. We must look for the *influence* of antichrist in our religious traditions: Are those traditions founded upon Scripture or upon man? And then, beyond our traditions, in the immediacy of our own hearts, we must discern the *disposition* of the antichrist spirit in the thought structure of our flesh nature. Is there something in your soul that opposes and exalts itself above God? The resistance in you against God is an idol. It is the most powerful idol in the human heart.

My Spiritual Preparation for Today

Day 83
Modern-Day False Gods

Therefore put to death the parts of your earthly nature: sexual immorality, uncleanness, inordinate affection, evil desire, and covetousness, which is idolatry.
—Colossians 3:5

The false god of self-rule does not stand alone in man. The ancient god Mercury would be hard pressed to keep pace with today's gods of anxiety and haste. The world has taken its bloodlust out of the ancient Roman arenas and put it into violent movies. They have taken the goddesses of fertility from the Greek hillsides, only to idolize sex in our theaters and on our televisions. What mankind has done is move the pagan temples from the high places of the countryside to the hidden places of the human heart.

If we exalt money, status, or sex above the Word of God, we are living in idolatry. Every time we inwardly submit to the strongholds of fear, bitterness, and pride, we are bowing to the rulers of darkness. Each of these idols must be smashed, splintered, and obliterated from the landscape of our hearts.

My Spiritual Preparation for Today

Day 84
God Is Jealous for Us

You shall not worship any other god, for the
Lord, whose name is Jealous, is a jealous God.
—Exodus 34:14

The Lord did not say He was, at times, jealous; He said *His name,* which reveals His *nature,* is Jealous. Right next to His name "I AM" is His name "Jealous." His love is not some ethereal principle of "higher cosmic consciousness." His love is focused upon us, actually jealous for us as individuals. He "calls his own sheep by name" (John 10:3). Jesus knows your name. He loves you personally. The fact that Christ is jealous for us as individuals, caring and providing for each aspect of our lives, and suffered humiliation and death on the cross to pay for our sins demonstrates how great a love it is with which He loves us. He gave all. He deserves all.

His jealousy for us is perfect. It is not the same as human jealousy: petty, possessive, and insecure. His jealousy is based upon His pure love for us and His desire to bless us and fulfill our lives in Him. He understands us, yet knowing our weaknesses, He refuses to stop loving us. You may think of yourself as a sinner, as unlovable—as though no one wants you—but Jesus desires you.

My Spiritual Preparation for Today

Day 85
GOD'S FAITHFULNESS

We know that the Son of God has come and has given us understanding, so that we may know Him who is true, and we are in Him who is true—His Son Jesus Christ. He is the true God and eternal life. Little children, keep yourselves from idols.
—1 JOHN 5:20–21

EARLY IN MY ministry, upon occasion I gave up on certain individuals, people who seemed to me hopelessly unreceptive to God. As the years passed, I would later discover these same individuals were now walking with God. Jesus is faithful. He loves you with a love that is jealous for you as a person.

God knows, however, that in order for you to *experience* His love, the idols of self and sin must be destroyed. And to prove our intentions and love for Him, *He tells us to smash these idols*. Would you be holy? Then remove the idols of self and sin from within you. For holiness exists in a soul purified by love; it exudes like incense from a heart without idols.

MY SPIRITUAL PREPARATION FOR TODAY

Day 86

Real Knowledge

For this reason also, since the day we heard of it, we have not ceased to pray for you and to ask that you may be filled with the knowledge of His will in all spiritual wisdom and understanding.
—Colossians 1:9, NASB

So much of our Christian experience is based upon the assimilation and digestion of knowledge. When we first come to Christ, our attention is devoted to having our needs met. Unfortunately our spiritual powers of discernment are underdeveloped. Instead of maturing in the Lord, often we are merely indoctrinated into the concepts of our first teachers—and not all those concepts are biblical.

If our knowledge about God is not charged with the life and power of God, mere knowledge becomes an idol in our mind. It is improbable that everything we have been taught since we first learned of Christ is from Christ. We must not allow our thoughts about God to become as unchangeable as God, for we are in transition, and there is much to learn, relearn, and forget. The Lord wants us to be rooted in Him, not rooted in our ideas about Him. We must be confident enough of His love to be able to uproot a wrong idea; an idol is an idol.

My Spiritual Preparation for Today

Day 87
UNTRUE IDEAS OF GOD

But our God is in the heavens; He does whatever He pleases.
—PSALM 115:3

YOU AND I both have ideas, images of God that are untrue, which the Holy Spirit would remove if we would let Him. These are cultural and doctrinal traditions that have become ingrained in our minds. The power of Christ's life is filtered and proportionally diminished by the number of these wrong images existing within us. Individuals, churches, and even nationalities superimpose their likenesses upon their concepts of God. Poor and rich nations alike suppose that the almighty Creator exists and thinks as they do. They are not serving God but the *image* they have of God. Yet the Living One is not a Caucasian or an African American. He is not a Greek or Jew, a Catholic or a Protestant. He is God! He does as He wants. We cannot "train" the Lord to think like an American. He is the sovereign Creator, the life source of the universe.

MY SPIRITUAL PREPARATION FOR TODAY

Day 88
THIS GOSPEL

And this gospel of the kingdom will be preached throughout the world as a testimony to all nations, and then the end will come.
—MATTHEW 24:14

IN MATTHEW 24 Jesus warned about the tremendous powers of deception that would be unleashed in the last days. He repeated His warning several times, saying many would be misled. But in the middle of His prophetic revelation, our Lord declared that the gospel, *just as Jesus taught it*, with its power to heal, deliver, and make men holy, will be proclaimed as a testimony just before the end comes (v. 14).

What is this gospel of the kingdom? *It is the whole message of Jesus Christ.* It is more demanding, more fulfilling, more holy, and more powerful than the "gospel" of typical American Christianity. Once found, it must be sought first, even before necessary food and clothing, and it is such a priceless treasure that one should rather suffer the loss of a hand or eye than lose the kingdom (Matt. 6:33; Mark 9:47). It is the gospel that costs us our all but gives us God's best.

And if we are listening to something that does not center us firmly upon the gospel as Jesus taught it and on the path into God's kingdom, if we are not becoming like Jesus in holiness and power, we are being misled.

MY SPIRITUAL PREPARATION FOR TODAY

Day 89

BIGGER THAN WE KNOW

Look, God is great, and we do not know Him, nor can the number of His years be searched out.

—JOB 36:26

THE KINGDOM OF God is not a religion; it is an ever-expanding, all-consuming relationship with Jesus Christ. It is as different from religion as a brilliant angel is from a shadowy ghost. If you think God is religious, always remember: there was no religion in Eden. The only temple God dwells within on the earth is the temple of our human bodies. John, in the Book of Revelation, is very plain. He says of Heaven, "I saw no temple in it" (Rev. 21:22, NASB).

Our thoughts about God being religious are just a sign we don't truly understand Him. The Father does not want us to worship or serve something so small that a human, finite mind could envision it. He is greater than our vision of Him. Knowledge is important, but it is merely symbolic; it is only a reflection of reality, never the substance. Our thoughts are helpful, but they are not comprehensive.

MY SPIRITUAL PREPARATION FOR TODAY

Day 90
Life Is Found in Christ

You search the Scriptures, because you think in them you have eternal life. These are they who bear witness of Me. Yet you are not willing to come to Me that you may have life.
—John 5:39–40

We often seek God through the Scriptures. Reading the Word of God is important, but know that our life does not come from the Bible; it comes from Jesus. Those who wrote the Bible wrote to bear witness of Him. The Old Testament prophets pointed forward to Him; the New Testament authors direct us back to Him. But if we would seek to actually understand what they wrote, we must find whom they found.

You see, we are not seeking knowledge through reading the Bible; we are seeking God! We are not hungering for facts but for fullness (Matt. 5:6). God is greater than man's knowledge of Him. If we truly have approached the living God, our knowledge will stand meekly in the shadow of awe and wonder.

My Spiritual Preparation for Today

Day 91
Seek the Lord, not Answers

To know the love of Christ which surpasses knowledge.
—Ephesians 3:19

Knowledge informs us that God is eternal, but *eternal* is just a word to us. What quality of life has He that the billions of years in the long, full circle of time have both their beginning and end in Him? Our doctrines tell us He is the Creator, but what kind of power exudes from Him that entire galaxies are created by His words, and by a decree from His mouth our earth teems with life? We define Him as omnipresent and omniscient, but can you describe with knowledge how He can be in every place at once, and how He could be fully conscious of each of us—even the numbers of hairs on our heads?

Our words about Him are infinitely inadequate to describe His real person. As we seek, it is important to understand that there is a difference between seeking answers and seeking the Lord. There is a difference between secondhand book knowledge and a firsthand encounter with the Living One. God must become as real, as full, and as all-consuming to us as the world was when we were sinners.

My Spiritual Preparation for Today

Day 92
More Than Our Knowledge

For as the heavens are higher than the earth, so are My ways higher than your ways, and My thoughts than your thoughts.
—Isaiah 55:9

The cry of our hearts must be, "Let God be God! Let Him be to us who He truly is!" Right knowledge is vital, but we want more than just knowledge. We want the presence of the Almighty to fill the vacuum of our doctrines with substance, the very substance of Himself.

There is a story about Saint Augustine that may help explain my point. Augustine, considered a great church father, lay on his deathbed at the end of his life surrounded by his most intimate friends. His breathing stopped, his heart failed, and a great sense of peace filled the room as he went to be with his Lord. Suddenly, he reopened his eyes; with his ashen face now flushed with light, he spoke, "I have seen the Lord. All I have written is but straw."

We may have ideas, we may possess fairly accurate scriptural knowledge, we may have had visions and dreams, but everything we think we know is but straw compared to the actual reality of the presence of God. The Lord is bigger, more wonderful, more powerful than the sum of everyone's knowledge about Him.

My Spiritual Preparation for Today

Day 93
Repent from Idolatry

Previously, when you did not know God, you served those who by nature are not gods. But now, after you have known God, or rather are known by God, how do you turn again to the weak and beggarly elemental forces to which you desire again to be in bondage?
—Galatians 4:8–9

We do not have to be great thinkers to understand that both sin and false knowledge can become idols. Why are we centering our thoughts and energies upon repentance from idolatry? Because, in the very place where the idols of self and false knowledge dwell, the living God has chosen to bring forth His presence. The true, eternal God cannot be alloyed with the false gods of this age. We cannot serve two masters. We cannot have His power and holiness in our lives without having Him in our lives. And if we are not being progressively transformed into His holy and powerful image, we may be serving an idol: the idol of false knowledge.

My Spiritual Preparation for Today

Day 94
Cleansing the Sanctuary

So they gathered their brothers together and consecrated themselves and entered in as the king commanded by the words of the Lord in order to cleanse the house of the Lord.
—2 Chronicles 29:15

How little we understand of the One who has granted us the unfathomable riches of His presence! We are called to be His house, His place of rest. Yet not until we are cleansed of sin will His purposes for us become clear. Indeed, it is the pure in heart who see God.

Within the heart of every Christian there is a secret place, a sanctuary we must prepare for the Lord. This holy place is not unlike the Holy of Holies in the Jewish temple. Not until this place is cleansed will the Lord dwell within us in the fullness of His Spirit; not until this room is pure will we truly become a house for the Lord.

My Spiritual Preparation for Today

Day 95
Open the Door

David says concerning Him: "I foresaw the Lord always before me, for He is at my right hand, that I may not be shaken."
—Acts 2:25

Just as Hezekiah reopened the temple doors for restoration, so also in us there is a door that we must open daily to the Lord (2 Chron. 29:3). David wrote that the Lord was always with him. Right there within the psalmist's heart was a dwelling place for the Lord; David was always beholding the Lord. Similarly, there is something in our presence, in our spirits, that can be opened or closed to God. We must not assume that because we are Christians this gate toward God is automatically opened. Jesus stood "at the door" of the church in Laodicea and knocked, desiring to enter their lives (Rev. 3:20). We must choose to unlock this door and swing it wide toward Christ.

My Spiritual Preparation for Today

Day 96

Know Him and Be Known

But if anyone loves God, this one is known by Him.
—1 Corinthians 8:3

OPENING THE CHAMBER of our hearts can indeed be a frightening thing. It requires that we be open to talk to God and to hear from Him as well. It is one thing for us to speak honestly with the Lord; it is quite another when He speaks without restraint to us. Therefore, the most essential commodity for stimulating revival is a tender, open heart before God.

Is the door of your heart opened toward God? Can the Spirit of Jesus Christ come in and speak with you? Are you defenseless to His voice? Can you sense both His pleasure and His displeasure? For us to become sensitive to divine realities, we must live with the door of our hearts open. It is impossible to do the will of God otherwise.

My Spiritual Preparation for Today

Day 97
DEEP CLEANSING

Who may ascend into the hill of the LORD? And who may stand in His holy place? He who has clean hands and a pure heart, who has not lifted up his soul to falsehood and has not sworn deceitfully.
—PSALM 24:3–4, NASB

IN THE NEW covenant temple, the church, it is our private, inner lives that need deep cleansing. We have inherited traditions that justify and reinforce darkness of soul within us. The revival that will turn a nation begins in the trembling unveiling of our hearts, in the removal of what is defiled and hidden within us.

I will tell you a mystery. It is in this very place, this chamber of our deepest secrets, that the door to eternity is found. If the Father is near enough to "see in secret," He is close enough to be seen in secret as well. If He has entered us, we can, in truth, enter Him. The key to entering the presence of God is intimacy, and intimacy is secrets shared. To ascend the hill of the Lord, to stand in the holy place, we must have clean hands and a pure heart; we cannot lift up our souls toward falsehood. At this door of eternity we must renounce those things hidden because of shame and, in humility of soul, receive Christ's cleansing word.

MY SPIRITUAL PREPARATION FOR TODAY

Day 98
Cleansing Process

Beloved, now are we children of God, and it has not yet been revealed what we shall be. But we know that when He appears, we shall be like Him, for we shall see Him as He is. Everyone who has this hope in Him purifies himself, just as He is pure.
—1 John 3:2–3

Our goal is not merely to be "good" but to see God and, in seeing Him, to do what He does. However, John tells us that he who seeks to see the Lord purifies himself just as God is pure (1 John 3:2–3). We can be assured that each step deeper into the Lord's presence will reveal areas in our hearts that need to be cleansed. Do not be afraid. When the Spirit shows you areas of sin, it is not to condemn you but to cleanse you.

My Spiritual Preparation for Today

Day 99
Seek Purity, See Yourself

Create in me a clean heart, O God, and renew a right spirit within me. Do not cast me away from Your presence, and do not take Your Holy Spirit from me.
—Psalm 51:10–11

My wife set herself apart to seek the Lord. Her cry during this time was, "Lord, I want to see You." As she sought the Lord, however, He began to show her certain areas of her heart where she had fallen short. She prayed, "Lord, this is not what I asked for; I asked to see You, not me." Then the Holy Spirit comforted her, saying, "Only the pure in heart can see God."

My Spiritual Preparation for Today

Day 100

The Glory of the Father

Then Jesus said to them, "Truly, truly I say to you, the Son can do nothing of Himself, but what He sees the Father do. For whatever He does, likewise the Son does. For the Father loves the Son and shows Him all things that He Himself does. And He will show Him greater works than these so that you may marvel."
—John 5:19–20

In the same way that the Lord desires us to see ourselves for who we really are, the Lord desires His church to see Him as well. Thus, He is exposing the areas in us that are unclean so that we can see Him clearly. If we will walk as Jesus walked, we must remember that Christ did only the things He saw the Father do (John 5:19). Out of the purity of His heart He beheld God and then revealed His glory.

We must cleanse the house of the Lord so that we might sincerely be prepared to seek and find the leading of God and, upon hallowing His presence, do what we see the Father doing.

My Spiritual Preparation for Today

Day 101
A Way of Life

The service of the house of the Lord was set in order. Then Hezekiah and all the people rejoiced that God had prepared the people, since the events happened suddenly.
—2 Chronicles 29:35–36

This cleansing process of the temple of God within us must become a way of life, but it does not have to take a lifetime. For Hezekiah and the people with him, it occurred in a matter of eight days.

The key here is this: the cleansing of the temple was the highest priority of the king's life. When we set our hearts toward true holiness, we too will rejoice over what God has prepared.

My Spiritual Preparation for Today

Day 102
Bringing Us to Glory

God has from the beginning called you to salvation through sanctification by the Spirit and belief of the truth. To this He called you by our gospel, to obtain the glory of our Lord Jesus Christ.
—2 Thessalonians 2:13–14

The Lord is cleansing us for the distinct purpose of bringing His people into His glory. Out of His desire to present a pure bride to His Son, the Father is purging the church of its sin. He is refusing to allow our interchurch relationships to continue without love. According to the Scriptures, before Jesus returns, the body of Christ will be holy and blameless (Eph. 5:27; Phil. 2:15; Col. 1:22; 1 Thess. 5:23; Titus 2:14). Through new and successive levels of purity, the house of the Lord will again see and reflect the glory of God.

My Spiritual Preparation for Today

Day 103
THE SOURCE OF HOLINESS

Therefore, if any man is in Christ, he is a new creature. Old things have passed away. Look, all things have become new.
—2 CORINTHIANS 5:17

WHILE THE WORD *holiness* means "to be set apart, separate," a possible interpretation of the Hebrew root word for "holiness" is "to be bright; clean, new or fresh; untarnished." Holiness produces separation from sin, but mere separation from sin cannot produce holiness. It is not the absence of sin that produces our sanctification; holiness comes from the presence of God. You may avoid touching what is unclean, but if you are not united through love to the fatherhood of God, you will never know true holiness; all you will have is religion. Christ in us is our holiness, for as close as our relationship is with Him, to that degree we reflect His holiness.

MY SPIRITUAL PREPARATION FOR TODAY

Day 104
RELIGIOSITY

Woe to you, scribes and Pharisees, hypocrites! You tithe mint and dill and cumin, but have neglected the weightier matters of the law: justice and mercy and faith. These you ought to have done without leaving the others undone.
—MATTHEW 23:23

JESUS WAS THE most holy man who ever lived, yet He was totally free from religiosity. What is "religiosity"? It is an attitude that emphasizes form and ritual as the standard of righteousness above pure attitudes of heart. The Pharisees are an example of religiosity.

Until the time just prior to the birth of Christ, the Pharisees were typically the most noble men in Israel. They were righteous, bold, and, upon occasion, martyred for their faith. But, like any sect whose religious emphasis is not motivated by compassion and love of God, the Pharisees' concept of separation eventually made them aloof and self-righteous toward their fellow man. By the time Christ was born, the Pharisees were proud of their image and the honors afforded them as clergy.

MY SPIRITUAL PREPARATION FOR TODAY

Day 105
Self-Righteousness

For, being ignorant of God's righteousness and
seeking to establish their own righteousness, they
did not submit to the righteousness of God.
—Romans 10:3

To illustrate how self-satisfied the Pharisees had become, look at the period of time surrounding the birth of Christ. Their indifference toward this momentous occasion is indicative of how distant they had grown from God and how preoccupied they had become with their religion. The Pharisees knew the Scriptures and were the heirs of the law of Moses, yet they showed no interest and sent no delegation when Christ was born, even they could have walked to His birthplace in less than three hours.

How immovable the Pharisees were from their self-righteous attitudes. How fearlessly they resisted the Spirit of God! Vigorously they held to their tradition; how carefully they maintained their image. Consider: on the night they crucified Christ, they refused to enter the Roman Praetorium "so that they might not be defiled" (John 18:28). They kept the details of the law while crucifying the Lawgiver!

My Spiritual Preparation for Today

Day 106

Hold Tight to God and Live His Word

Be doers of the word and not hearers only, deceiving yourselves.
—James 1:22

This was the Pharisees' religiosity: they held tighter to their doctrines than they did to God. They loved the audible praises of men more than the approval of the Almighty. They assumed that knowing the Scriptures was as weighty as living them. In short, *they acted like many Christians act today: more concerned with religion than with truly following Jesus.*

And so, before we judge the Pharisees harshly, let us measure ourselves: How do we compare in terms of justice, mercy, and faithfulness? How compassionate are we in our caring for the needy and giving ourselves to see the sinful changed? Indeed, Jesus warned that unless our righteousness exceeds that of the Pharisees, we cannot enter the kingdom of Heaven (Matt. 5:20).

My Spiritual Preparation for Today

Day 107
THE FRUIT

Either make the tree good and its fruit good,
or else make the tree corrupt and its fruit
corrupt. For the tree is known by its fruit.
—Matthew 12:33

Was Jesus talking about botany in the verse above? Of course not. Rather, He was speaking with reference to the essential nature of a thing. If you want to know if your doctrines are good, examine the fruit they produce in your life.

Christ's virtue and power came from the *Holy* Spirit, not a *religious* spirit. It was the fruit of the Holy Spirit that the Father crowned with power. Love healed broken bodies. Peace drove out tormenting spirits. Joy released captives from sin. The Holy Spirit in the life of a believer should produce a holy life.

My Spiritual Preparation for Today

Day 108
A Holy Life

But the fruit of the Spirit is love, joy, peace, patience, gentleness, goodness, faith, meekness, and self-control; against such there is no law.
—Galatians 5:22–23

What does a holy life look like? Just as a tree is known by its fruit, so the nature of the Holy Spirit is also revealed, or known, by its fruit; a holy life is seen in its fruit. If you think you are walking in the Holy Spirit, in discernment, in gifts, yet lack the love and joy and peace of the Holy Spirit, you may only be walking in a false religious spirit. If you are able to notice how "holy" you are becoming, you are not becoming holy; you are becoming religious. Holiness does not notice itself. Holiness is a tree laden with spiritual fruit, a tree rooted in the presence of God.

Indeed, where religion continues to splinter into divisions and strife, holiness—that is, the essential nature of God—brings forth fruitfulness, healing, and unity. How we need true holiness! For today we live in a world where church is divided from church and believer from believer. If the Holy Spirit were truly ruling, there would be repentance, healing, restoration, and love. There would be true and lasting miracles.

My Spiritual Preparation for Today

Day 109
Unity in the Church

Now I ask you, brothers, by the name of our Lord Jesus Christ, that you all speak in agreement and that there be no divisions among you. But be perfectly joined together in the same mind and in the same judgment.
—1 Corinthians 1:10

The separation we see in Christianity today is evil. It is a sin that needs to be repented of before Jesus returns. It is religious. There should only be one church in each community: a multifaceted church that, although it meets in different buildings, is yet united in Spirit and love with one another. And there will indeed be another group, a false church, comprised of various isolated camps of people who all presume they alone are right, people who call themselves "The Separate," never realizing that such is the name of the Pharisees.

Remember this: religion is its own god. Jesus never said we were to be "the denomination of the world," a "sect set on a hill." No. He said we were to be the "light of the world. A city [community] that is set on a hill" (Matt. 5:14). When you are holy, you will be more concerned with people than you are with religion; you will reflect the compassions of your King.

My Spiritual Preparation for Today

Day 110
Be Overshadowed by Glory

And Jesus called His disciples to Him, and said, "I feel compassion for the people, because they have remained with Me now three days and have nothing to eat."
—Matthew 15:32, NASB

There were two occasions when Jesus fed the multitudes. The first event occurred in a desolate region of the Judean wilderness, and it lasted one day. During the second event, the multitudes had been with Jesus for three days without food on a hillside near the Sea of Galilee.

The impact Christ had upon the local Jewish society was unprecedented! Their entire economy stopped. No one picked over or sold vegetables in the marketplaces, goats were not milked, gardens were left untended, and relatives watching little children did not know when the parents would return! For three days nothing at all was normal. These local communities left all when they heard Jesus was near. Without forethought, four thousand men, plus additional thousands of women and children, spontaneously followed Christ to a "desolate place." With all these people, we still read of no one complaining that the service was too long, the weather was too hot, or the message was boring. *Whatever they lacked in comfort and convenience was overshadowed by the glory of being with the Son of God.*

My Spiritual Preparation for Today

Day 111
His Kindness Leads Us to Repentance

Do you despise the riches of His goodness,
tolerance, and patience, not knowing that the
goodness of God leads you to repentance?
—Romans 2:4

A problem exists among many of us. People who do not really know Christ seek to represent Him to others. And instead of testifying of His wonderful works, they testify only of their religion. The unsaved do not see Jesus. They hear about church; they are told sin is wrong, lusts are evil, and drunkenness is a terrible shame, but they do not see the love of Jesus. Yes, these things are wrong, but *people must meet the love of Jesus before they will abandon their love of sin.*

My Spiritual Preparation for Today

Day 112
Be a Witness for Christ

Let your light so shine before men that they may see your good works and glorify your Father who is in heaven.
—Matthew 5:16

Jesus plainly called a number of people to silence concerning Himself. There were some whom He told, "See that you tell no one" (Matt. 8:4, also 9:30; 12:16). Others He outright forbade to speak, even though what they spoke was truth (Mark 3:11–12). Still others He warned would be doing great works, yet He neither sent them nor spoke to them, nor did He ever know them (Matt. 7:22–23). Indeed, there are those of whom He spoke whose zeal for converts takes them over "sea and land," yet their proselytes become "twice as much a son of hell" as they themselves are (Matt. 23:15). It is not our goal to discourage any from witnessing but to bring us to the realization that what we are in *attitude* and *deed* is the testimony that will be "known and read by all men" (2 Cor. 3:2). A "witness" is not just that which is "said"; it is also that which is seen. *If we will draw men to Christ in Heaven, they must be eyewitnesses of Christ in us.* But if we have flagrant sin or self-righteousness, our witness is noneffective.

My Spiritual Preparation for Today

Day 113
The Light of the World

In Him was life, and the life was the light of mankind. The light shines in darkness, but the darkness has not overcome it.
—John 1:4–5

Light, in the Scriptures, symbolizes the outraying purity of the holy God. When our hearts and subsequent actions are pure, the light of God's presence shines through us into this world. It is with this in mind that Jesus tells us to let our light shine before men in such a way that they see our good works and glorify the Father (Matt. 5:16).

My Spiritual Preparation for Today

Day 114
What Witness Do We Show?

Let no unwholesome word proceed out of your mouth, but only that which is good for building up, that it may give grace to the listeners.
—Ephesians 4:29

If goods works glorify the Father, then bad works bring Him dishonor. Paul tells us that "the name of God is blasphemed among the Gentiles" because of the sins of those who fail to represent Him (Rom. 2:24).

King David was a great witness of the living God to his generation, but when David sinned, his witness became a reproach. In Psalm 51, David's prayer reveals the right attitudes necessary to truly witness for God. He prayed, "Create in me a clean heart, O God, and renew a steadfast spirit within me.... *Then* I will teach transgressors Your ways, and sinners will be converted to You" (Ps. 51:10–13, NASB, emphasis added). You see, the credibility of our witness is lost when sin rules in our lives. The world has heard too many Christians give testimony to a life they are not living. They cause multitudes of people to think Christianity does not work.

My Spiritual Preparation for Today

Day 115
Live for Him

But sanctify Christ as Lord in your hearts, always being ready to make a defense to everyone who asks you…for the hope that is in you, yet with gentleness and reverence.
—1 Peter 3:15, NASB

Many Christians are told to witness for Jesus. Again, I would not discourage your witness for Jesus; rather we seek to *encourage* you to live for Him as well! Let people see Him in you before you testify. There are Christians who publicly sin in the workplace: they lose their tempers and do bad work; they are often late or heard complaining about management and job conditions. Yet they feel compelled to give their testimony. "They profess to know God, but by their deeds they deny Him" (Titus 1:16, NASB).

There is one sure way to know if the "voice" urging you to witness is from God: if the voice speaking to you is the *audible* voice of someone who has seen your good works and is asking about your way of life, that voice has been inspired by God. When people see Christ in you—in your patience when wronged, your peace in adversity, your forgiveness amidst cruelty—they will ask about your hope.

My Spiritual Preparation for Today

Day 116
Let Love Be a Witness

By this all men will know that you are My disciples, if you have love for one another.
—John 13:35

If your conversion is genuine, you found a love for Jesus that is, in itself, a witness of His life. Unfortunately we often seek to lead people into our religion instead of to Christ. How often we seek to convert our family and friends into a particular church structure. People must be led to Jesus, not merely to church.

Let us always remember, Jesus wants to reach people, not drive them away. How does God expect us to do that? First, let us make sure our conversion is real, that we have truly given over our lives to Jesus Christ. Then, determine to bear the spiritual fruit of love and humility in your life.

My Spiritual Preparation for Today

Day 117
THE FRUIT OF THE TREE OF LIFE

On each side of the river was the tree of life, which bore twelve kinds of fruit, yielding its fruit each month. The leaves of the tree were for the healing of the nations.
—REVELATION 22:2

IN THE GARDEN of Eden the Lord placed trees with seed in the fruit. *Remember this always: the power to reproduce life is in the fruit.* And for fruit to be edible, it must be mature and sweet. The fruit we must display comes from the tree of life, which brings "healing of the nations" (Rev. 22:2). It is not in the tree of the knowledge of good and evil—legalistic laws, judging what is wrong in people.

If you would like to see reproduced in your loved ones or friends the experienced reality of God, walk in the fruit of the Spirit. The power of reproduction is in the seed, and the seed is in the fruit.

And should you sin or stumble before them, which we all do at times, repent both to God and to those you have sinned against. A sincere repentance to an unsaved person is a sure sign that God is both real and in control of your life!

MY SPIRITUAL PREPARATION FOR TODAY

Day 118
Bear Fruit

I am the vine, you are the branches. He who remains in Me, and I in him, bears much fruit. For without Me you can do nothing....My Father is glorified by this, that you bear much fruit; so you will be My disciples.
—John 15:5, 8

Parents, do you want your children raised for Christ? Do you want your words to impart eternal life? Walk in the fruit of the Holy Spirit. As the fruit in your life nourishes your children, the seeds within your fruitfulness will reproduce in your family the same qualities. Would you convert your spouse? Your parents? Your friends? Walk in the fruit of the Spirit, in love, joy, peace, patience, and kindness. Those who know you will find your life very attractive, for through your life they will see the holy life of Jesus.

Jesus, let me abide in You. Let me cling closely so I bear fruit, and let that fruit attract people to You. Amen.

My Spiritual Preparation for Today

Day 119
Love Others

You shall love your neighbor as yourself.
—Mark 12:31

Most of us are afraid to live in the exposed, vulnerable state of heart that love demands. As Christians, we talk about love much more often than we live it. But real love is daring; it is exciting. It boldly conquers evil, then heals and reunites with God those whom it loves. It is aggressive.

The state of love of which we are afraid is that transitory stage where we are learning to forgive. This is the aspect of love that hurts, and its hurt is amplified by our reluctance to forgive. We, like Jesus, must live in a continual attitude of forgiveness; then we can step into the joy and power of aggressive love.

God's love is not just forgiving; it is for living. As we overcome bitterness and climb out of the pit of unforgiveness—suddenly we are as bold as a lion. Love grows from being a commandment to becoming an adventure!

My Spiritual Preparation for Today

Day 120
The Joy of the Lord

Do not be grieved, for the joy of the Lord is your strength.
—Nehemiah 8:10

The joy that comes to us through the Holy Spirit is a joy that actually becomes our strength! The imprisoned, impoverished state of this world has deceived us into thinking that a life with God is only a life of pain. Jesus compared His ministry to one who "played the flute" (Matt. 11:17). He said His message of grace and the kingdom of God, when it was properly heard, should cause men to "dance" in celebration!

It is true that Jesus suffered in bearing our sins and that there were times of great sobriety when He spoke. But there were many other times when He exhibited great joy. The Scriptures tell us that Jesus "rejoiced greatly in the Holy Spirit" when His disciples returned from a powerful time of evangelism (Luke 10:21, NASB). How do you envision Jesus rejoicing? The word *rejoice* that is used here meant "to leap much for joy." Jesus, the King, was leaping for joy! So can we live in joy, even when life is hard.

My Spiritual Preparation for Today

Day 121
The Way of Holiness

A highway will be there, a roadway, and it will be called the Highway of Holiness. The unclean will not travel on it, but it will be for him who walks that way, and fools will not wander on it. No lion will be there, nor will any vicious beast go up on it; these will not be found there. But the redeemed will walk there, and the ransomed of the LORD will return and come with joyful shouting to Zion, with everlasting joy upon their heads. They will find gladness and joy, and sorrow and sighing will flee away.
—ISAIAH 35:8–10, NASB

BEHOLD THE WAY of holiness! Sorrow and sighing flee away! The highway to holiness is the way to *God,* not religion. Nowhere in the verses do we see any of the gloom hell forecasts for the godly. It is a way of life in which all the judgments, negative consequences, and problems of the sinful, unclean life—those things that brought death into our world—are eliminated from our lives! No unclean...no lion...no vicious beast will be found there. Much of the spiritual warfare that fed upon our ignorance, unbelief, and sinfulness is simply nonexistent for the holy.

My Spiritual Preparation for Today

Day 122
EVERLASTING JOY

Instead of your shame you shall have double honor,
and instead of humiliation they shall rejoice over their
portion. Therefore, in their land they shall possess
a double portion; everlasting joy shall be theirs.
—ISAIAH 61:7

WHAT IS IN store for those who walk toward holiness? It is the wonderful, experienced knowledge that we are "redeemed…and the ransomed." What attitude fills our hearts? Three expressions of joy await God's holy ones: "joyful shouting," "everlasting joy upon their heads," and "gladness and joy" (Isa. 35:9–10, NASB).

Satan would have us believe Heaven is as gloomy as hell. As we embrace holiness and walk in it, as we strive to live out lives consecrated in heart and mind unto God and separate from the lusts of the world, the Lord crowns us with everlasting joy. Not gloom—joy! Not "sometimes-lasting" joy but everlasting joy; not "Sunday-morning-only" joy but moment-by-moment, eternal joy!

This is no pious sense of religiosity; it is abounding in life. They "shout for joy over their portion" (Isa. 61:7, NASB)! This is the end result of holiness. It is nearness to God; it is joy worth shouting about and full of glory!

MY SPIRITUAL PREPARATION FOR TODAY

Day 123
For Our Good

We know that all things work together for good to those who love God, to those who are called according to His purpose. For those whom He foreknew, He predestined to be conformed to the image of His Son, so that He might be the firstborn among many brothers.
—Romans 8:28–29

The Lord has not promised us a world without hardship, but that, in the midst of hardship, He will be revealed through us.

What is God's primary purpose for us? Why were we created? From the beginning of time God created man with one purpose: to make us in His image according to His likeness. The Lord has never changed His divine intent toward us. Indeed, Paul tells us that God causes all things in our lives to work toward the good of this one eternal goal (Rom. 8:28–29). What of the difficulties and tribulations that we encounter in this life? In the scheme of God's plan, troubles and afflictions are upgraded to classroom lessons where we learn to appropriate the nature of Christ. Thus our difficulties compel us toward God, and He compels us toward Christlikeness and change.

My Spiritual Preparation for Today

Day 124
Do Not Be Afraid

Do not fear, for I have redeemed you; I have called you by your name; you are Mine. When you pass through waters, I will be with you. And through the rivers, they shall not overflow you. When you walk through the fire, you shall not be burned, nor shall the flame kindle on you. For I am the LORD your God, the Holy One of Israel, your Savior.
—ISAIAH 43:1–3

WHILE GOD'S PLEDGE in Isaiah is a great encouragement, we should be mindful that the Lord did not say He would keep us from the fire or the floodwaters, but He would be with us in them.

Why does the Lord allow us to pass through conflict in the first place? Because it is here that He trains His sons and daughters in Christlikeness. Recall the story of Jesus's disciples when they were without Him on a turbulent sea (Matt. 14:22–33). Their boat had been battered by the heaving waves and contrary wind. Jesus, walking on the water, came to them sometime in the early morning. His first words were those of comfort when He said, "Be of good cheer. It is I. Do not be afraid" (v. 27).

My Spiritual Preparation for Today

Day 125
I AM

Immediately Jesus spoke to them, saying,
"Be of good cheer. It is I. Do not be afraid."
—Matthew 14:27

The words Christ uses in His assurance of the disciples when they were afraid, "It is I," are translated other places within Scripture as "I AM." This phrase is the divine appellation—the eternal designation of God. While Jesus indeed comes to the aid of His disciples, He also reveals Himself transcendent of time's barriers. As such, He proclaims His availability to all His disciples. He is God with us, even to the end of the age!

Thus, Jesus still comes to His disciples' aid, manifesting Himself in the storms of our times, defying what seem to be impossible conditions in order to reach us. He is the master of every human distress; He can help us in every circumstance. In fact, this very setting of raging wind and sea is the classroom that the Son of God seeks to perfect His disciples' faith.

My Spiritual Preparation for Today

Day 126
Jesus Perfects Us

He said to her, "Woman, where are your accusers? Did no one condemn you?" She said, "No one, Lord." Jesus said to her, "Neither do I condemn you. Go and sin no more."
—John 8:10–11

Let us affirm the Father's highest purpose for us: Jesus did not come simply to console us in our fear but to perfect us! This is exactly where He will take us once we are willing. To behold Christ's goal of perfection for us is to truly gaze into another dimension of God.

We should repent of carrying the image of a Savior who fails to confront our sin or challenge our unbelief, for such is a false image of God. If we are to genuinely know Him, we must accept this truth: Jesus Christ is irrevocably committed to our complete transformation!

My Spiritual Preparation for Today

Day 127
Moments of Weakness

When Peter got out of the boat, he walked on the water to go to Jesus. But when he saw the strong wind, he was afraid, and beginning to sink, he cried out, "Lord, save me!" Immediately Jesus reached out His hand and caught him, and said to him, "O you of little faith, why did you doubt?"
—Matthew 14:29–31

When Peter walked on water, he did not rest his weight on the water; he stood on Christ's word: "Come!" Peter trusted that if Jesus told him to do the impossible, the power to obey would be inherent within the command.

Moments later Peter's faith faltered. He began to sink. But there is something extraordinary to be seen in Christ's response—a view into Christ's actual nature and His ultimate purpose. Jesus did not commend or congratulate Peter. He rebuked him!

Was Jesus angry? No. The truth is, Jesus Christ is relentlessly given to our perfection. He knows that wherever we settle spiritually will be far short of His provision. He also knows that the more we are transformed into His image, the less vulnerable we are to the evils of this world. Thus He compels us toward difficulties, for they compel us toward God, and God compels us toward change.

My Spiritual Preparation for Today

Day 128
GIVE OF YOURSELF

Heaven is My throne and the earth is My footstool. Where then is a house you could build for Me? And where is a place that I may rest?
—ISAIAH 66:1, NASB

GOD ASKS FOR nothing but ourselves. Our beautiful church buildings, our slick professionalism, all are nearly useless to God. He does not want what we have; He wants who we are. He seeks to create in our hearts a sanctuary for Himself, a place where He may rest.

In the Scriptures this *rest* is called "a Sabbath rest" (Heb. 4:9, NASB). It does not, however, come from keeping the Sabbath, for the Jews kept the Sabbath but never entered God's rest. The Book of Hebrews is plain: Joshua did not give the Israelites rest (vv. 7–8). And after so long a period of Sabbath-keeping, Scripture continues, "So there remains a Sabbath rest for the people of God" (v. 9, NASB).

MY SPIRITUAL PREPARATION FOR TODAY

Day 129
SABBATH REST

Then God blessed the seventh day and sanctified
it, because in it He rested from all His work.
—GENESIS 2:3, NASB

THE QUESTION MUST be asked then, "What is this Sabbath rest?" In Genesis God rested on the seventh day. Before God rested on the Sabbath, there was nothing special or holy about the seventh day. Had the Lord rested on the third day, then it would have been holy. Rest is not in the Sabbath; it is in God. Rest is a prevailing quality of His completeness.

Revelation 4:6 describes the throne of God as having before it, as it were, "a sea of glass like crystal." A sea of glass is a sea without waves or ripples, a symbol of the imperturbable calm of God. Let us grasp this point: the Sabbath was not a source of rest for God; He was the source of rest for the Sabbath. As it is written, "The Creator of the ends of the earth does not become weary or tired" (Isa. 40:28, NASB). And even as the Sabbath became holy when God rested upon it, so we become holy as we put away sin, as the fullness of God settles and rests upon us.

MY SPIRITUAL PREPARATION FOR TODAY

Day 130
Tremble at His Word

For My hand made all those things, thus all those things have come to be, says the Lord. But to this man I will look, even to him who is poor and of a contrite spirit, and trembles at My word.
—Isaiah 66:2

In the kingdom, there are no great men of God, just humble men whom God has chosen to use greatly. How do we know when we are humble? When God speaks, we tremble. God is looking for a man who trembles at His words. Such a man will find the Spirit of God resting upon him; he will become a dwelling place for the Almighty.

My Spiritual Preparation for Today

Day 131
Be Enveloped with God

Do you not believe that I am in the Father and the Father is in Me? The words that I say to you I do not speak on My own authority. But the Father who lives in Me does the works.
—John 14:10

The Hebrew word for *rest* is *nuach*; among other things, it means "to rest, remain, be quiet." It also indicates a "complete envelopment and thus permeation," as in the spirit of Elijah "resting" on Elisha, or when wisdom "rests in the heart of him who has understanding." God is not looking for a place where He can merely cease from His labors with men. He seeks a relationship where He can completely envelop and thus permeate every dimension of our lives, where He can tabernacle, remain, and be quiet within us.

When God's rest abides upon us, we live in union with Jesus the same way He lived in union with the Father (John 10:14–15). Christ's thought life was completely enveloped and thus permeated with the presence of God. He did only those things He saw and heard His Father do; it was the Father doing His works (John 14:10). There is rest because it is Christ working through us.

My Spiritual Preparation for Today

Day 132
God Works Through Us

I will do whatever you ask in My name, that the Father maybe glorified in the Son. If you ask anything in My name, I will do it.
—John 14:13–14

God works through us when we ask Him. How vain we are to think we can do miracles, love our enemies, or do any of the works of God without Christ doing the works through us! This is why Jesus said, "Come to Me...and I will give you rest" (Matt. 11:28). In a storm-tossed boat on the Sea of Galilee, Christ's terrified disciples came to Him. Their cries were the cries of men about to die. Jesus rebuked the tempest, and immediately the wind and sea became "perfectly calm," even as calm as He was (Matt. 8:26, NASB). What program, what degree of ministerial professionalism can compare with the life and power we receive through Him?

You see, our efforts, no matter how much we spend of ourselves, cannot produce the rest or life of God. *We must come to Him.* Many leaders have worked themselves nearly to exhaustion seeking to serve God. If they spent half their time *with Him,* they would find His supernatural accompaniment working mightily in their efforts.

My Spiritual Preparation for Today

Day 133
Enter the Lord's Rest

For whoever enters His rest will also cease from his own works, as God did from His.
—Hebrews 4:10

To enter God's rest requires we abide in full surrender to His will, in perfect trust of His power. We learn to rest from our works as God did. To "rest from our labors" does not mean we have stopped working; it means we have stopped the laborious work of the flesh and sin. It means we have entered the eternal works that He brings forth through us.

The turmoil caused by unbelief is brought to rest by faith. The strife rooted in unforgiveness is removed by love. Our fearful thoughts, He arrests through trust; our many questions are answered by His wisdom. Such is the mind that has entered the rest of God.

My Spiritual Preparation for Today

Day 134
Knowledge Leads to Rest

"They have not known My ways." So I swore in My wrath, "They shall not enter my rest."
—Hebrews 3:10–11

The church needs to possess the knowledge of God's ways, for herein do we enter His rest (Heb. 3:8–12). We gain such knowledge through obedience to God's Word during conflicts. As we obey God through the testings of life, we learn how to deal with situations as God would. Consequently, it is of the utmost value to hear what God is speaking to us, and especially so when life seems to be a wilderness of hardship and trials.

Let us understand: *knowing God's ways leads to His rest.* We must see that there is no rest in a hardened heart. There is no rest when we rebel against God. Our rest comes from becoming honest about our needs and allowing Christ to change us.

My Spiritual Preparation for Today

Day 135
Learn From Him

Take My yoke upon you and learn from Me, for I am gentle and humble in heart, and you will find rest for your souls.
—Matthew 11:29, NASB

Stop fighting with God and learn from Him. Let His Word put to death the torments of the sin nature. Cease struggling, cease wrestling against the Blessed One. Trust Him! For eventually His Word will plunder the defenses of your heart. Be committed to your surrender. In time He shall no longer use adversity to reach your heart, for you shall delight in being vulnerable to Him. Continue your diligent yielding until even His whisper brings sweet trembling to your soul. Far more precious than the men of a hundred nations is one man perfectly given to the Spirit of God. This man is God's tabernacle, the one to whom God looks…and with whom He is well pleased.

My Spiritual Preparation for Today

Day 136
A Holy Place

"Heaven is My throne and the earth is My footstool. Where then is a house you could build for Me? And where is a place that I may rest? For My hand made all these things, thus all these things came into being," declares the Lord. "But to this one I will look, to him who is humble and contrite of spirit, and who trembles at My word."
—Isaiah 66:1–2, NASB

Incredibly, one man with one quality of heart captures the attention and promise of God. God looks to the man who trembles when He speaks. For in him the holy power of the Most High can, without striving, abide in perfect peace. He has learned the ways of God; he delights in obedience. He has chosen to give God what He asks: nothing less than all he is. In return, this man becomes a place, a holy place, where God Himself can rest.

My Spiritual Preparation for Today

Day 137
LIGHT

This then is the message which we have heard from Him and declare to you: God is light, and in Him is no darkness at all.
—1 JOHN 1:5

THE BOOK OF Psalms tells us that God covers Himself "with light as with a garment" (Ps. 104:2, NASB). James refers to the Father as "the Father of lights" (James 1:17). You and I are the "lights" that God has fathered. We are children of God, and, as such, the light of His presence shines within us. As our hearts are purified by truth, the splendor of God's glory expands around us, and like our Father, we also cover ourselves "with light as with a garment."

When true holiness exists in a Christian's life, it produces a luminosity, a glow around that individual. Infants and little children, because their spirits are yet pure and undefiled and because they are so close to the actual presence of God, emanate this light as well. Their light is visible because their hearts are transparent and truthful. For us, the way to the bright lamp of holiness is this same way of transparency and truth. It is the way to the pure gold of the kingdom of God.

MY SPIRITUAL PREPARATION FOR TODAY

Day 138

Seek the Fulfillment of Sanctification

But we all, seeing the glory of the Lord with unveiled faces, as in a mirror, are being transformed into the same image from glory to glory by the Spirit of the Lord.
—2 Corinthians 3:18

From the moment Christ enters within us, we are holy, set apart unto God. This kind of holiness is the same sanctification that made the utensils in the temple holy: holy because they were used in service to the Lord. They had no virtue in themselves; their material substance did not change. Christianity, in general, is holy in that sense. But the holiness we are seeking is the *fulfillment* of having been set apart. We are seeking a holiness that mirrors, through us, the presence of God in Heaven. We are seeking both His nature and His quality of life.

My Spiritual Preparation for Today

Day 139

The Spirit in Us

For as many as are led by the Spirit of
God, these are the sons of God.
—Romans 8:14

Since true holiness produces in us the actual life of the Holy Spirit, we must be sure we know who the Spirit is. The Spirit of God is love, not religion. God is life, not rituals. The Holy Spirit does more in us than simply enable us to "speak in tongues" or witness. *The Spirit leads us into the presence of Jesus.* Herein is our holiness received: in our union and fellowship with Jesus Christ.

Again, the holiness we are seeking is not a legislative or legalistic set of rules; it is Christ's very own quality of life. The Holy Spirit works in us not merely a new desire to love, but He imparts to us Christ's very own love. We develop more than just a general faith in Jesus; we actually begin believing *like* Jesus, with *His* quality of faith. It is *God in us* that makes us holy. Let it stagger us; let it rock us off our comfortable little perches until, with great trembling and great joy, with deep worship and holy fear, we approach the divine reality who has, for His own will and purpose, called us to Himself.

My Spiritual Preparation for Today

Day 140
THE TEMPLE OF GOD

Do you not know that you are the temple of God,
and that the Spirit of God dwells in you?
—1 CORINTHIANS 3:16

THE SPIRIT OF God dwells in us. In this light let us ask ourselves again the age-old question, "What is man?" We know how we appear to other men, but if God truly is within us, how do we appear to angels or devils? What light marks us in the spirit world? What illumination surrounds us? What glory declares to the invisible realm, "Behold and beware, here walks a son of God"? Think of it: the Spirit of the Creator, who purposed in the beginning to make man in His image, is in you...now.

MY SPIRITUAL PREPARATION FOR TODAY

Day 141
Who Do You Serve?

The eye is the lamp of the body. Therefore when your eye is good, your whole body also is full of light. But when your eye is bad, your body also is full of darkness. Take heed therefore lest the light which is in you is darkness.
—Luke 11:34–35

There are limitations. There are conditions. You cannot serve two masters. You cannot serve light and darkness, sin and righteousness, self and God. Light is within you, but so also is darkness. Our world is a world in darkness. Our ancestors were sons of darkness. Our carnal minds yet remain theaters of darkness. In a world of choices we must choose light. That is why Jesus taught that we must be single-minded if we would become fully mature sons of light.

If you are focused in your will and heart toward God, your body is full of light, and you are giving full expression to the glory of God within you. But if you are double-minded, if you are dwelling on sinful or evil thoughts, your light is proportionally diminished until your very body is full of darkness.

My Spiritual Preparation for Today

Day 142
Hope in the Light

If therefore your whole body is full of light, with no dark part in it, it will be wholly illumined, as when the lamp illumines you with its rays.
—Luke 11:36, NASB

If you do nothing about your salvation, fail to seek God, or choose to disobey Him, you are in darkness. Do not console yourself with an aimless hope that someday, somehow you will get better. Arm yourself with determination! For if the light in you is in darkness, how terrible is that darkness. Son of light, you must *hate* darkness! Darkness is the substance of hell; it is the world without God.

But our hope is light, not darkness. Your feet are walking the path of the just, the path that grows brighter and brighter unto the full day. The verse above gives a very clear picture of what holiness looks like in its maturity: our bodies are radiant with glory even as a lamp shines at full brightness. What a tremendous hope—that we can be so wholly illumined with the presence of God that there is "no dark part" within us. A garment of light and glory awaits the spiritually mature, the holy ones of God, a garment similar to what Jesus wore on the Mount of Transfiguration.

My Spiritual Preparation for Today

Day 143
CHILDREN OF LIGHT

For you were formerly darkness, but now you are Light in the Lord; walk as children of Light...Do not participate in the unfruitful deeds of darkness, but instead even expose them; for it is disgraceful even to speak of the things which are done by them in secret. But all things become visible when they are exposed by the light, for everything that becomes visible is light.
—EPHESIANS 5:8, 11–13, NASB

NOW YOU ARE *a child of light.* These are not merely figures of speech. The glory of God is within and around you; it is a spiritual reality! But what of the darkness that is yet within you?

Do not hide your darkness; expose it. Do not sympathetically make excuses for it; confess it. Hate it. Renounce it. For as long as darkness remains in darkness, it rules you. But when you bring darkness out into the light, it becomes light. When you take your secret sins and boldly come unto the throne of God's grace and confess them, He cleanses you from all unrighteousness (1 John 1:9). If you sin again, repent again—and again, until the habit of sin is broken within you.

MY SPIRITUAL PREPARATION FOR TODAY

Day 144
Stake Your Claim

I counsel you to buy from Me gold refined by fire, that you may be rich, and white garments, that you may be dressed, that the shame of your nakedness may not appear, and anoint your eyes with eye salve, that you may see.
—Revelation 3:18

Like the prospectors of old, you must stake your claim high in the kingdom of God, being ready to defend your rights to the pure gold of Heaven (Rev. 3:18). And as you pitch your tent at the throne of grace, something eternal will begin to glow in you, like hot coals on a furnace floor. And as you persist with the Almighty, the sacred fire of His presence will consume the wood, hay, and stubble of your former ways. Power such as Jesus had will reside in your innermost being. Angels will stand in awe, for your gold will be refined, your garments light, and your life holy.

My Spiritual Preparation for Today

Day 145
CHRIST'S DWELLING PLACE

Christ may dwell in your hearts through faith.
—EPHESIANS 3:17

THE BOOK OF Hebrews is a message to people who were familiar with the tabernacle of God and the significance of the Divine Presence in the inner court of the tabernacle. There are similarities between the inner and outer courts of the Hebrew tabernacle and the "inner and outer courts" of the New Testament tabernacle: *the Spirit-filled disciple*. Both have a sacred place that was created for the presence of God. And both have a prescribed way to enter the sacred presence.

There is a place in your spirit, in the sacred place, where Christ actually dwells, an abiding place where His Holy Spirit and your human spirit literally touch, as with the Hebrew tabernacle. You are eternally saved not because you accepted the religion called Christianity but because you have accepted the actual Spirit of Jesus Christ into your heart. Through Him you are able to come to God.

MY SPIRITUAL PREPARATION FOR TODAY

Day 146
Dwell Here

Examine yourselves, seeing whether you are in the faith; test yourselves. Do you not know that Jesus Christ is in you?
—2 Corinthians 13:5

The Bible is full of statements about Christ dwelling in us. In addition to 2 Corinthians 13:5, there is this passage: "Do you not know that you are a temple of God and that the Spirit of God dwells in you?" (1 Cor. 3:16, NASB). And again, Jesus, speaking for both Himself and God the Father, promised, "If a man loves Me, he will keep My word. My Father will love him, and We will come to him, and make Our home with him" (John 14:23).

Such statements are so bold that most Bible teachers refuse to deal with them for fear of being accused of heresy. Yet the incredible reality of God's Word cannot be altered in spite of compromise within the church. The holy meaning of the Word stands towering above men's traditions and unbelief. There is an "upward call of God in Christ Jesus" (Phil. 3:14, NASB). We will not ignore or rush past any of God's words. Rather, we encourage you to take time with this study, to dwell in it. For if you receive it properly, a door will swing open before you into the secret place of the Most High.

My Spiritual Preparation for Today

Day 147
The Outer Room

The Holy Spirit is signifying this, that the way
into the holy place has not yet been disclosed
while the outer tabernacle is still standing.
—Hebrews 9:8, nasb

The idea that we are saved because of our acceptance of the Spirit of Jesus into our hearts is not merely a doctrine of faith; it is a matter of fact. The dwelling of Christ in our spirits is a holy place. But how do we gain access to this holy place? The Book of Hebrews provides us with an answer: the way to the holy place is not revealed as long as the outer tabernacle is still standing.

What is this "outer tabernacle"? For the Jews, the outer tabernacle was the larger of the two rooms in the sacred tent. This room contained the lampstand, the table, and the sacred bread, and it was where priests entered as they ministered the daily worship service (Heb. 9:2, 6). A second inner room was also in the tent. It is this inner room that the high priest entered just once a year (v. 7). This was the Holy of Holies, the dwelling place of God on the earth. In this room dwelt His manifest presence.

My Spiritual Preparation for Today

Day 148
Let God Rule Your Life

Humble yourselves under the mighty hand of
God, that He may exalt you in due time.
—1 Peter 5:6

The outer and inner rooms of the Jewish tabernacle symbolize our own outer and inner natures. Our "outer tabernacle" is our soul life, constituting the view of life as seen through the mind and emotions (the soul) of man. In the tabernacle of our soul, our focus is outward. Worship consists of something we "perform." It is that part of us that keeps us in church because of duty rather than vision. It leads us by our traditions rather than the Spirit.

Rarely, if ever, does one experience the actual presence of the living God in the outer tabernacle. We may be saved by *faith*, but by *experience* the presence of God seems far removed. What is experienced is a myriad of different ideas, emotionalism (or lack thereof), and much confusion concerning church order, eschatology, and systems of worship. As long as man is ruled by circumstances rather than God, his "outer tabernacle" is still standing. No matter how zealous he seems, until the strength of his outer man is broken and an inner desire to worship and know God arises, the way into the holy place remains hidden.

My Spiritual Preparation for Today

Day 149
Come to the Father Through the Son

Jesus said to him, "I am the way, the truth, and the life. No one comes to the Father except through Me."
—John 14:6

Continuing the parallels between the Jewish tabernacle and human nature, the Bible tells us there was also an "inner tabernacle," which the Scriptures call the "Holy of Holies." This inner tabernacle corresponds to the spiritual side of man. As it was in the physical temple, so it is in the temple of flesh; the presence of God dwells in the inner tabernacle.

In the physical temple, the inner tabernacle was so sacred that no one casually entered the holy place. The manifested presence of Yahweh, God of Israel, dwelt in this sacred room. When we think of entering the reality of God's presence, we are immediately confronted with the depth of our sinfulness.

Yet for us, the way into this holy place is not through self-improvement or any similar vain attempt. We enter the presence of God through our identification with Jesus Christ. Most Christians place this promise in the hereafter. However, Jesus came to reconcile us to God in the *here and now* as well.

My Spiritual Preparation for Today

Day 150

DISCOVER THE ALMIGHTY ONE

For through Him we both have access
by one Spirit to the Father.
—EPHESIANS 2:18

THE WORD PROCLAIMS that we are "a holy temple in the Lord, in whom [we] also are being built together into a dwelling of God in the Spirit" (Eph. 2:21–22). We are God's holy temple, His habitation in the Spirit. And it is "access...to the Father," in which the Eternal One actually communes with us, that we are seeking.

Jesus said the Father is seeking worshippers. The worship that fully satisfies God must originate from the Holy of Holies, where the consciousness of man is awakened to the Spirit of God. Worship does not come from any system or form of service. Rather, it is the result of having truly discovered the Almighty One in "spirit and truth" (John 4:23).

MY SPIRITUAL PREPARATION FOR TODAY

Day 151
Separation From the Father

Nevertheless when anyone turns to
the Lord, the veil is removed.
—2 Corinthians 3:16

Because of sin and shame, every man places some sort of barrier between God and himself. The Bible refers to three instances of a veil separating the Jews from God. Paul talks of the third veil, less perceptible than the others and therefore more dangerous. This is the veil that remains unlifted, not only from the hearts of the Jews but also from all who know not God (2 Cor. 4:3–4). This is the veil mentioned in 2 Corinthians 3:16.

This third veil is the veil of our self-life. When the veil of self cloaks our hearts, our perceptions are stained by the basic selfish orientation of our nature. But when one turns to the Lord, the veil of self-life, like the veil in the temple, is rent in two. This is not the cutting of cloth but the rending of the heart, the splitting in two of the tightly woven fabric of self-righteousness and self-consciousness. It is a violent rending, a putting to death, of the unregenerated self-nature.

My Spiritual Preparation for Today

Day 152

The Sacred Presence of Christ

But we all, with unveiled face, beholding as in a mirror the glory of the Lord, are being transformed into the same image from glory to glory, just as from the Lord, the Spirit.
—2 Corinthians 3:18, NASB

Only if the old self-life is crucified without mercy or regret can the soul reach the state of purity where it begins to perceive, at last, the reality of God. In Moses we see a man *unveiled* before the presence of God. When Moses returned to the sacred tent, he would remove the veil from his face, turn, and step through the curtain of veils into the brilliant glory of God. Here, the Scriptures tell us, in the radiance of Eternal Life, Moses spoke to God face-to-face.

In like manner, *the very same sacred presence now dwells in the inner tabernacle of our spirits.* In Christ, with our veils of self, sin, and shame rent open, we too can turn and face God's glory—only the glory we face is not outside us. Nor does it fade from our faces as we depart from it. The Spirit of God dwells within us. And every time we truly behold Him, every time He is revealed to us, our hearts change in unending degrees of glory, transforming us into His same divine image from glory to glory (2 Cor. 3:18).

My Spiritual Preparation for Today

Day 153
THE VEIL OF CHRIST

Therefore, brothers, we have confidence to enter the Most Holy Place by the blood of Jesus, by a new and living way that He has opened for us through the veil, that is to say, His flesh.
—HEBREWS 10:19–20

IN THE LIGHT of such staggering spiritual realities, it is no wonder Satan fights the fulfillment of God's Word. The Father has provided a perfect offering, a sacrifice that for all time satisfies the penalty of sin. He has supplied an offering that enables us to enter the holy place through Jesus into His glorious presence (Heb. 10:20).

You see, the final veil through which we pass is not made of linen; it is the fleshly body of Jesus Christ. We return to God through Him. The Scriptures tell us, "If we confess our sins, He is faithful and righteous to forgive us our sins and to cleanse us from all unrighteousness" (1 John 1:9, NASB).

MY SPIRITUAL PREPARATION FOR TODAY

Day 154
FORGIVEN AND CLEANSED

My little children, I am writing these things to you that so you may not sin. And if anyone sins, we have an Advocate with the Father, Jesus Christ the righteous; and He Himself is the propitiation for our sins.
—1 JOHN 2:1–2, NASB

IT IS THROUGH Jesus's blood sacrifice that we are perfectly forgiven and thoroughly cleansed as we enter the presence of God. When Christ was resurrected, He entered into "the greater and more perfect tabernacle, not made with hands, that is to say, not of this creation" (Heb. 9:11, NASB). When Jesus entered this true heavenly tabernacle, of which Moses's tabernacle was a copy, He did not take the blood of goats and calves; He took His own shed blood into the holy place (vv. 12–14).

MY SPIRITUAL PREPARATION FOR TODAY

Day 155
The Heavenly Tabernacle

Therefore even the first covenant was not inaugurated without blood. For when every commandment had been spoken by Moses to all the people…he took the blood of the calves and the goats, with water and scarlet wool and hyssop, and sprinkled both the book itself and all the people, saying, "This is the blood of the covenant which God commanded you." And in the same way he sprinkled both the tabernacle and all the vessels of the ministry with the blood. And according to the Law…all things are cleansed with blood, and without shedding of blood there is no forgiveness.

—Hebrews 9:18–22, NASB

Under the old covenant, Moses sprinkled the blood of sacrificed animals upon everything in the holy place. *Through the sprinkled blood he cleansed the basic uncleanness that exists in all created things.* What Moses did through the sprinkling of blood in the earthly tabernacle, Jesus has done for us with His own blood in the heavenly tabernacle.

My Spiritual Preparation for Today

Day 156
Jesus's Life for My Redemption

Therefore it was necessary for the copies of the things in the heavens to be cleansed with [blood], but the heavenly things themselves with better sacrifices than these. For Christ did not enter a holy place made with hands, a mere copy of the true one, but into heaven itself.
—Hebrews 9:23–24, NASB

Apart from you and me, there is nothing else in the heavenly tabernacle that is defiled. *We are the "heavenly things" that needed cleansing with Christ's blood before we could enter the true tabernacle.* As Moses cleansed the earthly copy of the holy place with blood, so Jesus cleanses the people who enter the true tabernacle with Him in Heaven.

During the Passover meal Jesus took the symbolic cup of wine and told His disciples, "Drink from it, all of you; for this is My blood of the covenant, which is poured out for many for forgiveness of sins" (Matt. 26:27–28, NASB). Hebrews tells us this sacrifice was so perfect that "by one offering He has perfected for all time those who are [being] sanctified" (Heb. 10:14). When Jesus agreed to die for man, essentially what He said to the Father was, "Every time they sin and for every kind of sin they commit, as long as there is repentance and faith in their hearts, My life is given for their redemption."

My Spiritual Preparation for Today

Day 157
TRUE WORSHIPPERS

Yet the hour is coming, and is now here, when the true worshippers will worship the Father in spirit and truth. For the Father seeks such to worship Him. God is Spirit, and those who worship Him must worship Him in spirit and truth.
—JOHN 4:23–24

THE CALL AND desire of God is for our worship to be in spirit and in truth. *Through the provision of Jesus Christ, we can be as close to God as our desires will take us. The limits are not on God's side but on ours.* With transcendent wonder and holy fear we can bow and worship in the reality of His majesty. Through Jesus, we can draw near to God with a sincere heart in full assurance of faith; we can actually enter and abide in the holy place of God.

MY SPIRITUAL PREPARATION FOR TODAY

Day 158
See Clearly

In the midst of the throne, and around the throne, were four living creatures covered with eyes in front and in back.
—Revelation 4:6

Our purpose in reading the marvel spoken of in Revelation is not to spend ourselves in speculations about these creatures. Our goal is to possess that purity of heart that comes from living in the awareness of God. We're seeking the open vision that is manifested at His throne.

Though these "living creatures" may represent many things, one thing is certain: John was not seeing a nightmarish vision of six-winged beasts with dozens of eyes covering their bodies. What John saw was a symbol of a deeper truth. The many "eyes" represent the open, all-inclusive vision that is the result of being in God's presence.

My Spiritual Preparation for Today

Day 159
Heavenly Places

He raised us up together with Him [when we believed], and seated us with Him in the heavenly places, [because we are] in Christ Jesus, [and He did this] so that in the ages to come He might [clearly] show the immeasurable and unsurpassed riches of His grace in [His] kindness toward us in Christ Jesus [by providing for our redemption].

—Ephesians 2:6–7, AMP

Let it be known, where the Lord is, there also is His throne. If you've had a meeting with the Lord, it is because your spirit is at His throne. When you were spiritually reborn, you were born again "from above" (John 3:3, AMP). At this very moment, through the agency of the Holy Spirit, your spirit is "seated" with Christ upon His throne in heavenly places (Eph. 2:6). Where His presence is, there also is His throne; where His presence is, there also is open vision.

My Spiritual Preparation for Today

Day 160
SEEING GOD CLEARLY

In the midst of the throne, and around the throne, were four living creatures.... The four living creatures had six wings each, and they were covered with eyes all around.
—REVELATION 4:6–8

THESE "LIVING CREATURES" are symbols of the life we find as we abide in God's presence. In Him our eyes can *think*: they see with discernment and understanding. The mind of Christ fuses with our vision, revealing what was impossible to be seen by the narrowness of our perception; we see "in front and behind" (Rev. 4:6, NASB). Our vision also comes from "the center...[of] the throne" (v. 6, NASB). Not only do we see distant spiritual realities, but we are also close enough to penetrate and search the depths of God Himself (1 Cor. 2:10).

MY SPIRITUAL PREPARATION FOR TODAY

Day 161
See Yourself Clearly

The four living creatures had six wings each, and they were covered with eyes all around. All day and night, without ceasing, they were saying: "'Holy, holy, holy, Lord God Almighty,' who was, and is, and is to come."
—Revelation 4:8

In the same way that being near to God helps us to see Him more clearly, being near to God also gives us "eyes . . . within," eyes that monitor the motives that guide self, inner eyes that stand guard against sin (Rev. 4:8, NASB). The more our vision opens up, the greater we see God in His holiness. The slightest sin in our lives becomes significant; we are compelled to live pure and holy before Him.

The creatures at the throne of God do not cease to say, "Holy, holy, holy, Lord God Almighty" (Rev. 4:8). Day and night, God is holy. When our spiritual eyes are open, the utterances of our mouths are all, "Holy, holy, holy."

My Spiritual Preparation for Today

Day 162
No Deceit!

Jesus saw Nathanael coming to Him, and said of him, "Behold, an Israelite indeed, in whom there is no deceit!" Nathanael said to Him, "How do You know me?" Jesus answered and said to him, "Before Philip called you, when you were under the fig tree, I saw you." Nathanael answered Him, "Rabbi, You are the Son of God; You are the King of Israel."

—John 1:47–49, NASB

What kind of man was Nathanael, a young disciple, that *Jesus* should praise him? There was no guile, no deceit in this young man's heart. Oh, how we should desire this purity for ourselves! Nathanael had "eyes...within," as Revelation references (Rev. 4:8, NASB). He kept himself free from self-deception. *When you cleave to the truth inwardly, you will perceive the truth outwardly.* Nathanael did this as He declared that Jesus was the Son of God (John 1:49).

My Spiritual Preparation for Today

Day 163
OPEN VISION

"You will see greater things than these." And He said to him, "Truly, truly, I say to you, you will see the heavens opened and the angels of God ascending and descending on the Son of Man."
—JOHN 1:50–51, NASB

NATHANAEL HAD JUST proclaimed Jesus to be the Son of God. Because of Nathanael's honest heart, Jesus knew open vision was inevitable for Nathanael. Open vision is the consequence of a pure heart. To those who fight against sin, who hate falsehood, who diligently pursue walking in holiness, your struggle is a preparation for seeing God. You shall see the heavens opened.

MY SPIRITUAL PREPARATION FOR TODAY

Day 164

Are We Spiritually Blind?

"In the last days it shall be," says God, "that I will pour out My Spirit on all flesh; your sons and your daughters shall prophesy, your young men shall see visions, and your old men shall dream dreams."
—Acts 2:17

Because of our dullness of heart, we have come to expect spiritual blindness as an unfortunate condition of this world. The truth is, in the Old Testament one of God's judgments against sin was that the heavens became "bronze." Most Christians similarly see the heavens closed. Few see with open vision either into the heavenly realms or into their own hearts. *The heavens are always "bronze" to a hardened heart.* But the Lord promised, "You will see the heavens opened and the angels of God" (John 1:51, NASB).

God wants us to have true spiritual vision. One sign that the Holy Spirit is involved in a church is that young men see visions and old men dream dreams (Acts 2:17). *There is continuity between God's kingdom in Heaven and His kingdom on the earth.*

My Spiritual Preparation for Today

Day 165
We See the Eternal

While we do not look at things which are seen, but at the things which are not seen. For the things which are seen are temporal, but the things which are not seen are eternal.
—2 Corinthians 4:18

Oh, there are those who say the supernatural was strictly limited to the first century, that today "we walk by faith, not by sight" (2 Cor. 5:7). Yes, we often do take steps of faith, where we walk without prior knowledge of what each step involves. *But we do perceive Him who is with us!* Ours is not a blind trust; it is a proven, seeing trust! Walking by faith and having spiritual vision is not an either/or situation. Paul did both, and so can we. Paul had *revelation perception of the spirit realm.* He saw the eternal spiritual body that was prepared and waiting for him in the heavens (2 Cor. 5:1, 4)!

My Spiritual Preparation for Today

Day 166
A Pure and Holy Heart

Therefore, having these promises, beloved, let us cleanse ourselves from all defilement of flesh and spirit, perfecting holiness in the fear of God.
—2 Corinthians 7:1, NASB

We can continue discussing Paul's spiritual perception, but the fact is, he authored one-third of the New Testament out of his open vision of Christ. How did he see the things he saw? Just after he declared, "With unveiled face [we behold]…the glory of the Lord" (2 Cor. 3:18, NASB), he wrote, "But we have renounced the secret things of shame" (2 Cor. 4:2). Later he continued on to say that because of these promises of God, we should cleanse ourselves and live in holiness (2 Cor. 7:1). Out of a purified heart, out of his perfected holiness, came open vision of the glory of God.

My Spiritual Preparation for Today

Day 167
Seek a Pure Heart

Blessed are the pure in heart, for they shall see God.
—Matthew 5:8

Remember, we are not seeking experiences; we are seeking a pure heart. We are not running after visions; we want holiness. Even as the supernatural realm was an expected phenomenon in the primitive church, so also was purity the expected condition in their hearts. Therefore do not be as the foolish ones who seek visions. You must seek sanctification, and when you are ready, if God wills, He shall speak to you in supernatural ways (Acts 2:17–18). Do not seek to conjure up an "experience" with Jesus; seek to have a clean heart, allowing Christ to examine and purge you daily. And as He washes you with His Word and chastens you with His holiness, He will draw you into His presence.

My Spiritual Preparation for Today

Day 168
Set Apart

I urge you therefore, brothers, by the mercies of God, that
you present your bodies as a living sacrifice, holy, and
acceptable to God, which is your reasonable service of worship.
Do not be conformed to this world, but be transformed
by the renewing of your mind, that you may prove what
is the good and acceptable and perfect will of God.
—Romans 12:1–2

We are called to become a holy bride, the spotless wife of Jesus Christ. But before we become a bride, we must first become a virgin. In the Bible a virgin was not just one who was free from the sins of premarital sex or immoral behavior; a virgin was also one who was set aside for another. The sense in which the church is to become virginal involves being uncorrupted, pure, and undefiled by the world. It implies being untouched by man's ideas, traditions, or sinfulness. To reach the goal of spiritual virginity, we must first be perfectly consecrated, wholly set apart for Jesus (2 Cor. 11:2–3).

My Spiritual Preparation for Today

Day 169
Imparted Holiness

Blessed be the God and Father of our Lord Jesus Christ, who has blessed us with every spiritual blessing in the heavenly places in Christ, just as He chose us in Him before the foundation of the world, that we would be holy and blameless before Him.
—Ephesians 1:3–4, NASB

Like everything in true Christianity, the purity of the church is not that which originates from herself; it is that which is imparted as virtue from Christ. It is true, living virtue, but it is Christ's virtue. Jesus, you will remember, was also a virgin. He had set Himself aside for us, and He imparted His holiness to us.

My Spiritual Preparation for Today

Day 170
The Union of Christ

For this reason a man shall leave his father and mother and shall be joined to his wife, and the two shall become one flesh. This mystery is great; but I am speaking with reference to Christ and the church.
—Ephesians 5:31–32, NASB

This passage is in reference to Christ's union with the church, the marriage ceremony of the Son of God and man. Christ and His church: the *two* become *one* flesh! The apostle said, "This mystery is great" (Eph. 5:32, NASB). Do not presume you understand this just because you can read. This mystery is *great.* Jesus left His positional privileges as God's Son and clothed Himself in human flesh so that, through our spiritual rebirth, He might absorb mankind into His nature: the two became one! Jesus will always be the Son of God, but in love He chose to cleave unto His wife, the church. And while He is forever one Spirit with the Father, He is forever *married* to the church. Indeed, has this not been the eternal purpose of God: to bring the Spirit of His Son into the church, thereby creating man in both the divine image and the divine likeness (Gen. 1:26)?

My Spiritual Preparation for Today

Day 171
From Adam to Christ

So it is written, "The first man Adam was made a living soul." The last Adam was made a life-giving spirit.
—1 Corinthians 15:45

Scripture calls Jesus Christ the last Adam (1 Cor. 15:45). He is the firstborn of the new creation as Adam was the firstborn of the old creation. The first Adam, however, in cleaving unto Eve, fell with her in sin. But Christ, in cleaving unto His church, has redeemed us and raised us up, seating us with Him in the heavenly places (Eph. 2:6).

The marriage of Adam and Eve, where Eve literally emerged and was born out of Adam's substance, is a prophetic type of the church born out of the actual substance of Christ. Paul tells us that our *bodies* are the physical members of Christ (1 Cor. 6:15; 12:12). We are not simply metaphorically the body of Christ, but spiritually we are "bone of [His] bones, and flesh of [His] flesh" (Gen. 2:23).

My Spiritual Preparation for Today

Day 172
CHRIST IN US

I have been crucified with Christ; and it is no longer
I who live, but Christ lives in me; and the life which
I now live in the flesh I live by faith in the Son of
God, who loved me and gave Himself up for me.
—GALATIANS 2:20, NASB

THIS TRUTH THAT we are in Christ is not New Age theology; it is not heresy. It is the unalterable Word of God. Christ Himself is *in* us. To believe otherwise is heresy. The test of Christian orthodoxy, according to Scripture, is in 2 Corinthians 13:5: "Test yourselves to see if you are in the faith; examine yourselves! Or do you not recognize this about yourselves, that Jesus Christ is in you—unless indeed you fail the test?" (NASB).

We must recognize this about ourselves: Jesus Christ is in us. Yes, it is heresy to say we are Christ. Yet it is also error to deny He is within us.

MY SPIRITUAL PREPARATION FOR TODAY

Day 173
CHRIST THROUGH US

Therefore, when He came into the world, He said: "Sacrifices and offerings You did not desire, but a body You have prepared for Me."
—HEBREWS 10:5

WHILE DESCRIPTIVE OF Christ's first coming, the verse above is also applicable of His presence during revival. Christ Himself is in us. However, for Him to come forth *through* us, we must become a pure virgin. Revival comes as Christ prepares for Himself a people; as He is raised up within them, He draws all men unto Himself. Their Christ-likeness is a door through which Jesus Himself enters the world. For revival to come forth, there must be holy people through whom Christ can work.

MY SPIRITUAL PREPARATION FOR TODAY

Day 174
The Will of God

Previously when He said, "You did not desire sacrifices and offerings. You have had no pleasure in burnt offerings and sacrifices for sin," which are offered in accordance with the law, then He said, "See, I have come to do Your will, O God."
—Hebrews 10:8–9

Secure this thought in your mind: when the Spirit of Christ comes into the physical world, He must enter through a physical body. As was stated, the people or "body" Christ uses, of necessity, must be holy. They will have been prepared, set apart for Him beforehand. The purpose of that body is not to offer ritual sacrifices typical of the time and customs of the people. Rather, when Christ enters the world, through them, He repeats His eternal purpose: "I have come to do Your will, O God" (Heb. 10:7).

My Spiritual Preparation for Today

Day 175
Let God Prepare You

Though He was a Son, He learned obedience through the things that He suffered, and being made perfect, He became the source of eternal salvation for all those who obey Him.
—Hebrews 5:8–9

We must not despise the time of preparation. Jesus Himself lived for thirty years before He was revealed and empowered as the Messiah. Although Jesus was always the Son of God, He "increased in wisdom" (Luke 2:52). He could not learn of the kingdom of God in the rabbinical colleges of His day, neither could any man teach Him the mystery of the miraculous. All this had to come directly from the Father Himself. Jesus was always sinless and obedient, but Hebrews 5:8–9 tells us He had a process to go through before He was ready to do the work of the Father. The destiny the Father planned for Christ was something Jesus grew into, just as we must.

My Spiritual Preparation for Today

Day 176

Fulfillment of Preparation

Now when all the people were baptized, and when Jesus also had been baptized and was praying, the heavens were opened, and the Holy Spirit descended in a bodily form like a dove on Him, and a voice came from heaven which said, "You are My beloved Son. In You I am well pleased."

—Luke 3:21–22

In the unfolding of Christ's earthy life, there was a point *in time* when His Messianic calling was announced from Heaven. After the water baptism, while Jesus was praying, the Spirit descended visibly upon Him in power, Heaven opened, and out thundered the voice of the Father: "You are My beloved Son..." (Luke 3:22). And all those promises and dreams, prophecies and visions, the thirty years of learning obedience and becoming acquainted with grief, stood poised in perfect surrender, focused upon this one incredible moment in time: "...in You I am well pleased" (v. 22). Instantly the power of Heaven flowed into the spirit of Jesus, and the ministry of the Messiah was birthed.

The voice of God spoke to Jesus. The requirements and days of preparation were fulfilled, and the Father said to Jesus, "Today I have begotten You" (Heb. 1:5, NASB; 5:5, NASB).

My Spiritual Preparation for Today

Day 177

MARY, THE MOTHER OF JESUS

Mary said, "I am the servant of the Lord. May
it be unto me according to your word."
—LUKE 1:38

IN A SENSE, Mary, the mother of Jesus, also was "a body [God has] prepared" (Heb. 10:5). When Christ first entered our world as an infant, it was Mary whom God chose to give Christ birth. *Mary's life symbolized the qualities the church must possess to walk in the fullness of Christ.* She was humble, considering herself a bondservant of the Lord; she unwaveringly believed the word spoken to her (Luke 1:34–38). And Mary was a virgin. These traits qualified her to be used by God in carrying and giving birth to Christ.

MY SPIRITUAL PREPARATION FOR TODAY

Day 178

The Discipline of the Lord

"For whom the Lord loves He disciplines, and scourges every son whom He receives." Endure discipline; God is dealing with you as with sons. For what son is there whom a father does not discipline?...He does so for our profit, that we may partake of His holiness.
—Hebrews 12:6–7, 10

Our humble state as the Lord's bondslaves is but a preparation for the coming forth of Christ in our lives. Yes, we have been disciplined by the Lord. However, the goal of the Lord's disciplining and chastening is not merely to punish; He seeks to make us *chaste*: pure and spiritually flawless. Indeed, our purity, our spiritual virginity as the body of Christ, is nothing less than God Himself preparing us, as He did Mary, to "give birth" to the ministry of His Son. Even now, in the spiritual womb of the virgin church, the holy purpose of Christ is growing, awaiting maturity, ready to be born in power in the timing of God.

My Spiritual Preparation for Today

Day 179
Labor of the Church

A great sign appeared in heaven: a woman clothed with the sun, with the moon under her feet, and on her head a crown of twelve stars. She was with child and cried out in labor and in pain to give birth.
—Revelation 12:1–2

We live within a time frame the Bible calls the "period of restoration" (Acts 3:21, NASB). Since the Reformation, the truth of Christ has been progressively restored to His church. Since the dark ages of apostasy, every time Christ's presence has been more fully revealed, it is because "a virgin church" has been in labor to bring Him forth. The Holy Spirit impregnates a Martin Luther or a John Wesley—a person who God knows will continually say yes to Him—with a vision of the living God. The vision spreads to others, where it is tested with persecutions and refined with fire, but it spreads. Yes, those people are flawed. Truly, not a one of them is perfect. But along the way their vision of God possesses their souls. They become the "woman clothed with the sun," the virgin church who is "in labor and in pain to give birth" (Rev. 12:1–2).

My Spiritual Preparation for Today

Day 180
THE CHURCH GOD HAS PREPARED

I have come to do Your will, O God.
—HEBREWS 10:7

AS HER HOUR nears, this virgin church lays aside her many tasks to focus on her one great commission. Through intense prayer and the agonizing of the Holy Spirit, in groanings too deep for words, she embraces her appointed destiny—until the very voice of Christ Himself is heard through her prayers: "Lo, I have come to do Your will, O God!" Birthed in His Spirit and in His power, fused together through love and suffering, this holy people become, as it were, a "body [God has] prepared."

Even now, hell trembles and the heavens watch in awe. For I say to you, once again the "virgin is with child."

MY SPIRITUAL PREPARATION FOR TODAY